The Correct Way To Fool Around
Part Three
By Jeremiah Dotson

TABLE OF CONTENTS

Acknowledgments

I would like to give an <u>exceptionally</u> large and overdue debt of gratitude to God for turning a three day, alcohol fueled rant, which became The Correct Way To Fool Around part one, into The Correct Way To Fool Around Part Two, Relationships - Pacification For Crazy People, Victims Of Circumstance and this, my fifth book; The Correct Way To Fool Around Part Three. Who knew so many people had such an interest in infidelity and deviant behavior?

I would also like to give an <u>exceptionally</u> large thank you to Kathy Keith, without
whom, much of my writing career would not be possible.

I would like to give a heart felt thank you, without <u>exception</u>, to everyone who
either purchased my books or took the time to read them. I do understand that some of my work could be interpreted as objectionable and this was never my intent. It's just that people need an outlet to sometimes vent their frustrations and often for me, that outlet was through my writing. The venting was not directed at any one person as much as it was more toward the game of infidelity itself. Infidelity can take a person to places a person should never go. It can make a person hate. It can make a person kill. When more people realize that infidelity is not just something you do, that it is something which needs to be handled with extreme care if handled at all, I believe fewer relationships would end because of it. Fewer lives would end because of it. My writing is just an attempt to have people understand that relationships will never be easy if people continue to think that they are. Everything worthwhile requires work. This includes a happy relationship. This includes a successful bout of infidelity. I sincerely hope that all who have delved into The Correct Way To Fool Around series will continue to do so. And as always, love the unbiased criticism – keep it coming! What I do not love however are the anonymous cowards who say things to the effect of 'your books aren't any good' without telling me why or the people who say

4

'your writing has no positive value' without reading any of them. I wish for these people to understand something – I am not, have never claimed to be and as far as I can see will probably never be a psychologist, psychotherapist or any of those people who claim to be 'experts' on folks and their relationships. I am just someone who enjoys writing about the crazy things I have seen and experienced. One of the main reasons I choose to put these incidents on paper – other than to provide an extreme amount of comic relief to people is so that at least a handful of folks will step back, take a look at their relationships and say 'hey, I can learn from the mistakes of somebody else.' I understand that there will always be some people who will be perturbed by the success of others and there will always be people who will hate those who tell the truth. I do not wish to make enemies. I wish to make people aware of what may be going on in their relationships. If people dislike me for telling the truth, I apologize, if people hate me for my success, however limited it may be, I apologize even more but the one thing I ask from everyone who has an opinion is that you read my material before you rush to judgment. Understand what it is you are commenting on before you start commenting. The title of this book does not mean I want anybody to go out and start cheating on their significant other. I want people to realize how widespread and hidden deception actually is. I want people to know that the relationship they have may not be the relationship they want. In short I want people to be aware.

I would also like to thank LW for being an <u>exceptional</u> bitch.

And finally, Mark & Corey – I Love You

Foreword

Throughout this book as well as throughout my other publications, I often use the term 'natural' or 'being natural.' What many people who read my books often do is assume that the definition of these words is the same definition, as the one they would give. My words are basically taken out of context and this is because too many people, instead of reading the entire book, will scan the table of contents, pick out the most intriguing chapter read it, and then make a determination on the entire book based on what was contained therein. This is quite often the problem. It is wrong to judge a book on one part or one word for that matter just as it wrong to judge a person on one part of their life. People think that by me saying it's natural for a man or woman to cheat, that I'm saying it is okay or forgivable. Nothing could be farther from the truth. I am not condoning unfaithful behavior nor am I making allowances for its existence. The term natural is nothing more than my personal description for the act of infidelity. Although most of what is contained in this and my other works is based on my personal experiences, there are a few instances and examples, which are the result of interviewing friends, acquaintances and random individuals. The women I've known and several of my friends, for the most part are the ones who inspired me to use the 'natural' term because many of them cheat so much, it just comes 'natural' to them.

Chapter One
Who Cheats More Men Or Women?

In the never ending struggle of our time, not the one of good against evil but man against woman, we are once again asked to examine who reigns supreme in the arena of infidelity. This question, besides being a guaranteed argument starter, is almost impossible to answer with anything other than speculation. Ask any man who has been in a relationship where his significant other has been caught cheating and he will more than likely say, 'women can't be trusted.' Ask this question of a particular woman and she will more than likely state the same about men whether she has been involved in an adulterous union or not. One of the biggest beliefs or should I say 'misconceptions' people have, is that men cheat more than women but women are supposedly better at cheating than men. (I'd really like to see those statistics!) I think this goes along with the old 'girls maturing faster than boys' belief. (And in response to that load of jaborwocky, girls do not mature faster than boys – they mature differently.) Anyway, I've noticed that people have this pre conceived notion about the female to male infidelity ratio because men in general, have what's called a lackadaisical mindset when it comes to capture. They, in a sense, care very little or don't care at all. Basically the belief among men is that cheating is a victimless and insignificant crime. A little sex here and there, as long as no sexually transmitted diseases arise, who does it really hurt? And if one of these men were to ever get caught, they would probably equate punishment with that of jaywalking. Believe it or not, jaywalking is an actual violation of certain statutes and ordinances but which law enforcement entities really care about it? Jaywalking is like many other infractions in life – as long as no one is hurt, the activities will most often be overlooked. This belief is fueled by the fact that not much value is put into the relationship to begin with or the fact that neither party complains. When people have something they don't completely care about, it is that much easier to rid themselves of that particular thing. This is one of the major reasons infidelity enters many relationships. If the initial interest or level of respect is not shared, the person with the lesser amount of interest can just go through the motions until something better comes along and when something better does come along, there will be very little stopping that person from being natural. Now even though women have been historically known for gossip, divulging secrets and general blabbing, some men are quite the 'women' when it comes to talking about their accomplishments. Men, in addition to having an abundance of the 'I don't care if I get caught cheating' mindset' feel they <u>must</u> inform someone if they have sex – they <u>absolutely must</u> inform someone if the person they had sex with is very attractive – and they <u>must absolutely, positively</u> inform another if they had sex with an attractive person while they were in a relationship. For many men, being unequivocally superior than another, is how they prove their self worth. Being able to say 'I have a better car, I have a better paying job or I have had more successful affairs than you' is what makes life for them worthwhile. Unfortunately, by certain men attempting to prove themselves, they are unwittingly giving off 'signs' that they are being natural more than they actually are. The bad part about this, other than the fact that infidelity itself has occurred or is occurring, is that people will often generalize those transgressions, giving the blame to many, based on the acts of a few. The arena of infidelity is the one place women are unusually quiet. There is little or no discussion about extra marital endeavors, hence giving credibility to the 'men cheat more' belief.

Another big belief or misconception is that men are supposed to be super resillient when it comes to their feelings, meaning when they get hurt - just like a little boy who falls off a bike, they are told to suck it up and get back on. Men are too often instilled with the belief that they are not supposed to cry. There is no 'come here, let me kiss the boo boo.' Unlike women who have focus groups and 'girls night out' as well as unlimited nights and weekends where they can talk and discuss and vent their anger toward men, men basically have to ignore whatever hurt they encounter. They are supposed to be tough as nails, at all times. This is good on the one hand because if men were to tear up every time a relationship ended, their masculinity would be severly questioned. What this belief often does is separate men from their emotions – causing them to be cold as opposed to being strong. This is bad on the other hand because in addition to them being seperated from their emotions, many times women feel that men are totally unfeeling, therefore those women are often hesitant to approach them when there is a problem in the relationship. The belief often is 'you're a man, you don't care' or 'you're a man, you don't understand.' Women, on the other hand too, are famous for that lifelong emotional crap, so much so that their feelings, when hurt, actually and wondrously have the capability to transcend to other women. Men get hurt in relationships and are expected to vent their anger and frustrations by simply sleeping with as many women as they can. (Not the worst remedy in the world but not exactly the best either.) Women get hurt in relationships and they supposedly have the right to be mad for years upon years. And all these women need to do is inform their 'female circle of influence' how much hurt one particular man has caused them and all of a sudden those girlfriends will start to believe all men 'ain't shit' to quote a few women I know. This belief or misconception comes about because many people become experts at hiding or manipulating feelings. Besides men historically not being able to cry, they are expected not to show emotion for fear of being classified as woman-like or gay. People cannot escape feelings because they are a part of life. What many people do however is suppress them – and not just by putting them away temporarily but by suppressing them almost to the point of non existence. They use this suppression technique for several reasons – from not wanting people to believe they're too nice to not allowing themselves to get caught up in relationships they know they or their partners are not ready for.

Many women have or are born with this maternal instinct or motherly type of unconditional love, which is automatically given to the men they deal with. This belief causes a lot of men to think that if one woman who is supposed to be so unconditionally loving and maternal, would betray them, then they all must be the same deep down inside. Most men have a widespread reputation for being dogs, so if and when a man is caught cheating, it is already expected and therefore many females are not completely devastated heart – wise. Other women who attempt to offer solace to their female compadres who have been in an affair tainted relationship may often do so by reciting that ever famous male bashing line; 'he's just being a man.' The women who say things like this usually fall into one of three catergories;

1) unhappy in their own relationships
2) not in relationships
3) not too much into men.

As far as the actual numbers of infidelity, I believe there are few correct statistics because most of the 'experts' who focus on this crime, focus on the perpetrators who actually get caught. There's a saying, which many criminals, cheaters and people with a low moral fortitude like to use to justify their actions. 'There's no crime unless a person is caught.' Using this type of logic, no one will ever be able to accurately predict how widespread or in whose favor the scales tip when it comes to cheating. Infidelity, if kept under wraps, can go on indefinitely. By using the methods of historical belief, meaning the belief that men are too dumb to catch women cheating and women are too smart to allow themselves to get caught, people will cheat forever because their partners won't too much worry about their actions. Plus with no one to tell except diaries and the computers of insecure people who need to prove themselves by keeping records, the amount of one's indiscretions can be as high as that person's level of prepration.

One of the things that i have noticed about some people's views on infidelity is that many of these people don't see their actions as wrong. Some of these people feel that their interaction with the opposite sex is nothing more than general interaction as long as no sex is being had. Now this belief is acceptable for the person not doing anything bad but what about the significant other? He or she may be aware that the other is keeping time with another but may be unaware of what is actually going on during those tmekeeping sessions. Now while nothing is in fact going on, the fact that one party does not know this for certain may make it seem as if something derrogatory is happening. This may make the wondering person unfairly accuse the other or it may make the wondering person begin to keep time with someone else as a precautionary measure. People drive the statistics on idelity wild sometimes because there are not enough cameras in this world. By this I mean that since the only absolutely true way to confirm if an individual is actually cheating is to find that person in the act of cheating. Many people are slick in that they can manipulate this by saying things to the effect of 'she's my friend' or 'he was just being nice.' Since infidelity for the most part takes place behind closed doors, people will never get the full picture, unless of course the parties commiting infidelity actually come clean and admit the indiscretion. This is why I say there should be a lot more cameras in this world because if there were, a lot more people would get caught in the act of infidelity. When people undertake the above methods; the 'she's my friend' and 'he's just being nice' many times they are lying to cover up the fact that infidelity has or is occurring. This is one of the ways in which people manipulate trust. They may already believe that a significant other is cheating but after hearing excuses which are meant to pacify, what could they really say?

Strip clubs, nude reviews and prostitution have historically been products, created for the enjoyment of men – thus leading to the belief that since men supposedly enjoy sex more than women, they will more aggressively pursue it, whether they are in a relationship or not. However as of late, women's enjoyment of these venues are rapidly catching and in some instances, surpassing that of men. The big belief is that women indulge in fantasies, which include things other than just sex, more than men. Men fantasize about sex (like that's a surprise to anyone) almost all the time. Often men focus on the act of sex itself, whereas many women focus on a particular individual with whom they desire to have sex. This is what can drive the potential cheating statistics haywire. What people don't always want to realize is that 'cheating' encompasses so many forms. For instance, there's the actual physical act, there is what some people call the emotional cheating thing (which I personally think is a high level of bull) and there is the viewing or thinking of the opposite sex in a less than platonic manner. This includes the indulgence of pornography, associations of a non physical, yet not completely platonic nature and wayward thoughts. Women and men both fantasize about sexual intercourse, whether it be with their lifelong partner or whether it be with some male or female stripper in the back of the club. The difference is that even though women's sexual desires can rival and sometimes surpass those of men, women are not supposed to be allowed to speak about them. Women are supposed to be wholesome and motherly and whatever else. The only accepted deviation from this type of belief is for those women of a certain type of late night employment. (Hookers!!!) Men far more often than women, act on their desires. This does not necessarily mean men cheat more, it means they are more likely to initiate an affair, which was the result of a 'fantasy.' Cheating, aside from the obvious bumping of uglies, can be little more than basic perception. Many people gauge infidelity by thoughts as well as actions – so depending upon an individual's classification of cheating, a person can be guilty of that charge one hundred to one hundred thousand times a day.

Chapter Two
How Not To Get Caught

In this world, there are several things, which unfortunately are nothing more than a part of life. Some of these things include weather, traffic and crime. They are unavoidable and for the most part unchangeable, especially crime. For instance, there are some countries like China, where monsoons are a common occurrence. The people who reside in these 'nice weather challenged' countries choose to accept the unstable weather and stay or not accept it and leave, if they have the means of course. There are some areas, like the Cross Bronx expressway, in New York, which no matter what time a person drives during the day, always seems to be crowded. Crime is the only real difference because no matter where you go, there will always be at least a miniscule level of criminal activity, which can't be avoided. The difference between crime and the weather & traffic is that with weather & traffic, a person can always leave at a different time or find a different route in which to avoid them. Crime, on the other hand, is everywhere. It has no forbidden zone nor does it have a time when it takes a break. I'd like to focus on crime for a second because crime and infidelity share many of the same attributes. Crime by definition refers to actions, which are forbidden by law, whether that law is federal, state, provincial or local. Infidelity refers to actions, which are forbidden by certain laws as well. Most times those laws are either moral or religious and if broken, have mental and or emotional consequences. Many states and municipalities provide severe legal penalties for breaking these laws too. There are people in this world who indulge in criminal activity like it's a part of their daily repertoire. These people are 'natural' but in a non sexual sense. They commit crimes so much, that that type of activity comes naturally to them. Now as easy as it is for some people to commit a crime, it is just as easy for others to figure out the specifics of how that crime may have been committed. People study certain crimes to get an idea of how to solve them, just as people in relationships who consistently get hurt, become proficient at what to look for in criminal matters of the heart – in other words, infidelity. In regards to being natural in the sexual sense, people have been known to unwittingly leave paper trails, computer trails and trails of every description, all because they don't give infidelity the respect it is due. This is what allows the people committing infidelity to get caught. The act of infidelity or being natural must be treated as if it were a child and not an abused child but a child who is loved unconditionally. Infidelity is fragile yet hypocritical. Fragile because like a child, if one does not pay close and constant attention to it, it will cause hurt to itself as well as possible hurt to the supposed caretakers. Infidelity is hypocritical because almost any man in this world will say 'I'll kill you if you cheat on any female member of my family' yet it's completely okay for that person to cheat on a female member of someone else's family. (Can anyone say double standard?) When people who are involved in infidelity ignore it or just let it straggle along without importance, detrimental things often happen. To elaborate a bit more on the above child example, if a person doesn't watch a young child while he or she takes a bath, there is a very strong possibility that he or she may scald him or herself or perhaps even drown. Letting a child use the stove to fix his food, without the proper guidance can lead to a loss of property or life, due to fire. Even allowing a child to drive a vehicle unsupervised can have deadly consequences. If infidelity is to grow, then it must be nurtured and protected. If not, it will cause at the very least, hurt feelings. People will and have many times before killed due to hurt feelings. The media is filled with stories of 'a married person is caught cheating, the spouse who catches him or her kills the cheater, the one he or she was cheating with, as well as himself.' Feelings are not always kept internally and cannot always be turned off and on as easily as some people make it seem. There are exceptions however, because a great many men temporarily turn off the feelings of hatred for a mother in law, if it is conducive to happiness in his relationship - but the hateful feelings of 'you cheated with my brother?' is not one of them. People who play this very dangerous game of infidelity can afford to be nothing other than extremely diligent in their efforts not to get caught. As history has repeatedly shown, there are many small things in this world, which will get people in trouble; to wit, a not too well thought out word or statement, a look, which lasts a second too long, even somebody wearing the wrong color in the wrong neighborhood. These are not massive acts of treachery, nor are they things, which are not easily forgivable. They are however things, which people hold in high regard. In many inner cities, if you stare at somebody, the perception will most likely be that you are attempting to initiate a fight. Nobody stops to think that maybe the person who is staring is just admiring the other's style of dress or particular hairstyle. People always hear the saying; 'everybody has a twin' yet no one stops to think that maybe they themselves resemble someone the staring person knows. How many times have there been police shootings because of mistaken identity? Too many to mention here. If a man were to call a woman a bitch, certain responses would occur and these responses would be due to several factors; for instance, if the man is in a relationship with this woman and the name calling was a precursor to sexual activity, the response might be beneficial. If, on the other hand a man were to call the wrong woman a bitch, chances are he would face repercussions from the woman and quite possibly her boyfriend and family. If a person were to wear the colors of one gang in another's gang's territory, it's possible that that simple action may cause that person's life to be put in jeopardy. The above were just a few examples of the things people hold in high regard. To some people, infidelity is the highest level of disrespect. Here's one of those crazy but true facts; People in this world will take their partners beating on them, they will take their partners staying out all hours of the night and some will even permit their partners to completely screw up their credit and good name but for some astounding reason or other, people lose all sense of reasonable thought when the idea of another entering their relationship, enters their head. What kind of scrambled logic or mixed up priority is that? That is an unfortunate reality, which exists in many relationships today. Men and women both have their own interpretations of love. Some of those interpretations, twisted as they may be, dictate that as long as a person's significant other does not cheat, everything else, which goes on in the relationship is tolerable and acceptable. This can be the equivalent to winning a multi million dollar lottery if this is the type of relationship a particular person desires. It can also cause the person who has this type of priority or mindset to lose his or her mind if they become involved with someone and that someone just happens to eventually cheat. It can do this by causing every other unpleasant memory or action that person may have committed to connect itself to the adultery or infidelity thereby causing the person with the twisted interpretations to completely lose what's left of their twisted mind.

To be successful at cheating (and remember **I'm not condoning, just informing**) a person has to be able to distance themselves from any possible connection between the person they are involved with and the third party involved in the affair. One of the best and simplest ways to alleviate the chances of getting caught is by not being seen in public with your natural partner **AT ALL**. Reason being, you never know who will be watching and you best believe someone will <u>always</u> be watching. People always tell me that they freely walk around with their natural partners and if they were to ever get caught or be questioned by their significant others, they would use one of the oldest and most universal excuses, 'that's my friend.' The friend excuse is a somewhat acceptable defense but the problem with that excuse is that even on those rare occasions when the line is actually true, who's really going to believe it? Reason being, that excuse is about as popular as 'honey, 'I've got a headache' when someone wants to get out of having sex. Everybody uses it. (If somebody really wanted to get out of sex with another, they would have to provide unquestionable proof that a legitimate reason for not wanting to do the do exists.) Not to get too much off the subject but one no-fail method for men to get around intimacy, for whatever reason is to take a cheap watch, one that you know will turn your wrist green and put it on Mr. Happy. Leave it there until the desired effect takes place. The lighter the individual, the better the result. Now if there's anyone out there reading this who actually has the gall to try this method, be aware that your significant other will probably drag your butt to the nearest hospital, subject you to a battery of tests and then, unless you come clean about your deception, will not have sex with you again until you can prove that you are not in any way contagious. This method may work for a person who has recently cheated and desires to temporarily get out of having sex with the ball & chain but the potential problems it may cause, may outweigh the potential benefits. Anyway back to being seen by your significant other, to alleviate or all together prevent even getting caught in that situation, avoid all outdoor contact with your natural partner. This includes never going to the store with them, never going to the club with them, never even going for a walk with them in the park. The main reason people get busted while being natural is because they don't give their partners credit for having a brain. They often think that since their partner is living on this cloud of complacency, meaning they think the significant other would never do anything wrong or anything to hurt them, they can flaunt their indiscretions in that person's face. What they do not realize is that <u>anytime</u> a couple is seen together, assumptions will be made. The assumptions can range from 'that's a happy couple' to 'she's just using him for his money' but there will be assumptions. If a person knows a couple is married and that person sees one of the couple with a member of the opposite sex, the biggest assumptions will be, that person of the opposite sex is either a family member, a mutual friend of the husband and wife or someone that person is having an affair with. It won't take but half a second for a person to pick up the phone and say 'I saw your husband with this woman at such & such place, at such & such time.' Yes, people are nosey like that. In my first book, The Correct Way To Fool Around, I suggested that if a person was observed in public with his or her natural partner, the best thing would be not to lie about being seen with the person but lie about why that person was in such close proximity. This lie is a 'good' thing to do to temporarily escape the immediate questioning but the 'bad' part about this 'good' thing is that, as with almost any other lie, sooner or later, it will have to be backed up and extended and prolonged. This is bad because as people age, the retention skills tend to be not as sharp as when people are young. If there is never a lie about somebody else to begin with, chances are there will never be a chance for memory lapse or trickery to trip a person up during questioning. Then again it should be stated that as people age, the fact that we forget things normally makes us more likely to confuse actual facts. If we don't try to remember and confuse dates, the fact that we try and remember but use the uh, I forgot excuse will make a suspicious partner doubt our stories even more. This is why I say if you are going to cheat on your significant other, make sure that everybody involved (except the significant other, of course) knows that the relationship is only to be about sex – no going out – no spending intimate evenings in public – just sex. Because if the only thing a cheater does is have sex, then the only thing a cheater will ever actually have to lie about is the fact that he or she had sex. There will never be any mix up of whether or not you and this person were at a club dancing together or whether or not you and this person were seen driving around in the family car. If you inform the significant other of the fact that you and the sex partner are going out before hand, the questions about whether or not you actually did will be limited. If you let the natural partner know to stick with the same story, things should be trouble-free. Everything else the cheater can admit to.

Another thing people in relationships fail to realize is that secrets will always be kept from the people they love. Those secrets may come in the form of anything from 'I had a sex change before you met me' to 'I'm cheating on you' but there are always secrets. Some secrets, especially those dealing with infidelity can be detrimental to a relationship. This is why a person must be diligent. This is why a person must sometimes be cold. There has to be an unchallenged level of understanding between both parties that the natural relationship must be preserved at all costs. If this means ignoring each other for days at a time, then this is what needs to be done. If this means not calling 'just to say hi' again, this is what must be done. It may seem cruel but it hovers somewhere near the same level of cruelness as walking into your multi level building late night and slamming the door in some stranger's face so as not to allow entrance to a possible rapist or psychopath. Cruel but necessary. By avoiding or at least limiting public contact, you will be lowering your chances of being seen. The lesser the amount of times a person is observed, the less the amount of times that person can be connected to doing something wrong. Remember there are some people in this world whose main purpose in life it seems, is to watch and report your comings and goings. These are the type of people who receive great pleasure in messing up your good thing. These are the people who love to see fights and hate to see others happy. The good thing about these people is that they are almost never in your relationship. The bad thing about these people is that they are everywhere and nowhere.

In a relationship, there will always be times when a couple will have to reinvent what gives each of them pleasure and happiness. If the relationship is one where there is deception and trickery, there will also be times when one or both of the parties in that relationship will have to reinvent methods to keep themselves from getting caught in the act of infidelity. One of those methods, which apply to both types of reinvention, is by employing the use of pictures. Pictures have been used since the invention of the camera to invite infidelity, prove infidelity or entrap guilty parties into admitting infidelity. On the side of the person wanting to have an affair with someone, the pictures can be an asset. For example, people who have expensive homes will often take pictures to show to others in the hopes that the others will be enticed into visiting. This technique works well with a certain type of mindset. Materialistic people who see an easy mark or who are intrigued by the prospect of quick monetary gain will often fall victim to this brand of trickery. What some people will do is show off what they have to attract others, who they know are not as affluent or well off as they themselves are. The less well off, materialistic people will say 'they've got something I want and I've got something they want.' The materialistic people will use their personal 'assets' (whatever they may be) to procure whatever it is they believe the more affluent people have. The popular thinking is if a person has a nice home or an extremely well furnished apartment, that person must have oodles of money. Pictures therefore can work to the advantage of both parties. On the side of the person who is wanted for the affair, the pictures can outline what that person my set their sights on. Pictures can work to the disadvantage of both parties as well. Let's say for instance a married or committed person is interested in a member of the opposite sex and that married or committed person lives apart from their significant other. Let's also say this married or committed person has not yet slept with the interested party but has shown the interested party pictures of the inside of his or her home. People don't realize how often and how easily they give others a peek into their lives. This could be accomplished by showing pictures of a child's birthday party to co workers at the office or by showing pictures of a single sibling to an interested single party. What may happen after a person sees these pictures is that that person may go to the spouse of the one who showed them the pictures and claim to have physically been in their home or in the home of the significant other. I know this can get a little confusing so I'll enlist the help of Kim, Ryan & Tasha. Let's say Kim & Ryan are married. They are both very well off and Tasha knows this. Ryan is interested in Tasha, who just happens to be a materialistic, money hungry, bitch. Ryan may use pictures of his assets to show to Tasha in the hopes that she will be so impressed, that her money grabbing, materialistic ways will expose themselves. Tasha may think that she can outplay Ryan by using her body to acquire whatever Ryan has shown her. On the other hand Tasha may have previously tried to acquire some of Ryan's assets and have been turned down. If Tasha has seen a picture of the inside of Ryan's home and she knows Ryan's wife, how easy would it be for her to mention to Kim that she has been in their home on a more than platonic visit. All Tasha would have to do is say to Kim that she & Ryan did it on the blue, white and brown living room couch and to corroborate her story, she could mention that there are three pictures of the kids on the living room wall or state where the television is positioned. If that's not a viable enough scenario, there is always the possibility of

Tasha living in the same apartment building as Ryan & Kim but on a higher floor. What if one day, while Kim was at work, Tasha knocked on Ryan's first floor apartment door to ask if she could use the bathroom because she didn't think she would make it all the way upstairs. Ryan, being the nice guy that he is, allows Tasha to enter not only his & Kim's apartment but their bathroom as well. Tasha could have used the bathroom as planned, and then brushed her hair with one of Kim's brushes before she left. Ryan may or may not immediately tell Kim that Tasha stopped by because maybe he forgot or maybe he didn't think that it was significant enough to mention. Maybe he doesn't tell Kim because he knows Kim has a suspicious nature. Whatever the case, all Tasha would have to do to create drama is say that she & Ryan had physical relations and then took a shower afterward. If Kim were to dispute the story, again Tasha could mention that she used the brown towel hanging on the rack, then brushed her hair with the black brush after she & Ryan showered together with the bottle of Happy Times bath gel, which was resting in the shower rack. If Kim goes home and finds hair in her brush, which is a different color or different length than her own, there will be problems. Anything that would make Kim believe Tasha was actually inside the house will add to the level of concern. Ryan could be the best husband in the world but if Tasha were to approach Kim with the above treachery, that would create doubt and doubt is all that is necessary to raise the level of suspicion. If the conversation between Kim & Tasha would ever get to that point, it would basically be a matter of he say – she say. If Kim has the type of trust that I believe all couples need in this world, she & Ryan can quickly get past this infidelity resembling situation but if Kim has a suspicious nature or prior reason for suspecting Ryan, then its curtains!

The one thing people who commit infidelity do not do, which continuously gets them busted is a proper and thorough clean up of the home after committing the act of infidelity. This means more than doing a step-by-step condom wrapper search. This means retracing every dirty, vile and immoral step, which was made during the transgression. The problem with many cheaters today besides the fact that they are cheating is the fact that they are lazy when it comes to the after transgression cleanup. Many of these people expect that whatever is out of the ordinary to be staring them in the face, plain as day. They pay little attention to detail. There are certain things a person must look for before the significant other gets home and has a chance to do so. Here's a popular example of how water can cause a person to get caught in the act of infidelity: Some people who live with their husbands or wives or significant others still like to have affairs in the home. Let me say again that this is not the ideal place or the wisest option when it comes to infidelity. Some of these people who commit indiscretions, after doing so, will shower, and then attempt to clean up the house. The thing, which causes these people to get caught, is the fact that they either take showers at an unusual time of the day or the fact that they don't completely towel dry the bathtub after doing so. Some people take showers every morning and night. Some people take showers before they go to work and some people take showers only before they go to bed. If a person who is known for taking showers morning and night, has a wet bathtub in their home during the afternoon, questions may be raised as to why. The significant other may come home early one day and see that a shower was taken and wonder if the other is preparing to go out or has just finished doing something, which would require a shower. What most people will do is after they have an affair in the home, take a shower, clean up the home to the best of their ability but let the bathroom air out on its own – not realizing that the tub may still be wet an hour later. The after sex shower droplets will sometimes leave a person, especially an inquisitive person with questions. <u>Questions lead to doubt and doubt leads to suspicion.</u> If the suspicion cannot be eradicated or suppressed in an appropriate or timely manner, the person causing the suspicion will be under the microscope for an indefinite period of time.

Not getting caught in the act of infidelity requires three things, planning, planning and more planning. This is the basic foundation for any successful venture in life. A well thought out strategy, which details the potential risks, as well as the potential rewards is part of any winning business plan. It's always good to have protection, such as condoms on hand or the morning after pill in case the condoms fail but a genuine 'what if' plan will supersede all else. When a person goes on a job interview, they need to be ready for any potential question their prospective employer may ask. One question, which is often asked but often overlooked by potential job seekers is the 'what type of job are you looking for?' Many prospective job seekers will assume that if the advertised or desired position is administrative assistant, then administrative assistant will be the appropriate answer to the above question. However answering a question in the above manner will show an employer an applicant's lack of preparedness. A proper or better answer would be 'I'm looking for a position, which offers open communication and clear objectives.' An answer such as this covers most questions employers are looking for because it tells the employer that the job seeker a position, which will allow him or her to be able to talk to whoever whenever the need so arises. It also tells the employer that the jobseeker desires a position, which lays the job and its duties out in a clear and concise manner. When a police officer goes out on patrol, he or she needs to be ready for any possible situation, which may present itself. This may be anything from a ten-year-old child with a gun to a daytime hostage situation. The cheater is no different. As I've mentioned before, there is no limit to the density of deception in relationships today. A person will use any lie, excuse or reason they can fathom to extricate themselves from an unfavorable infidelity type situation just as people will use any lie, excuse or reason to procure what they desire. People who have read my previous works often ask me what should they do if their significant other was to come home while they were entertaining their natural partner. I would first tell them only a fool, somebody who is hell bent on breaking up with their significant other or somebody with a death wish would entertain at home, especially if their significant other has a key. Second, I would tell them to always have on hand or always have their partner have on hand a pair of dark sunglasses, preferably broken and a fold up walking stick. These are two of the few things other than prayer, which may help you out of the 'my significant other came home and I had someone else in the house' thing. The dark glasses and folding stick are handy because they are something almost every blind person has or has had experience with. They are also handy because almost everybody has some level of sympathy for the blind. If you are about to start or have recently finished doing the do and you hear that unmistakable sound of your significant other coming in, just tell them the person is blind and was either lost or getting assaulted or something and you just decided to play good Samaritan and help. Make sure the 'blind' person knows about the scheme ahead of time so that they don't share the same bewildered look that your significant other is likely to have. Also make sure that the glasses and walking stick are in close proximity to where your natural partner will be because it will be kinda hard to explain why a blind person has their stick hidden in your bedroom. Most people, as mentioned before, will have immediate sympathy and will try to make the blind person as comfortable as possible. This is bad. The more time the 'blind' person is in the presence of your significant other, the more time your significant other will have to try and solicit information from them about their supposed attack. Not to mention, they may insist that you or they call the proper authorities and report the incident. This can trip you up because (worst case scenario) what if they do call the police and the police come to your home to take a report. What are you going to do if they say they were attacked at a location you have no business being - as in you live and work on the west side and on your way home you discovered a woman being attacked. You then jumped out of your car and scared off her attackers or if you're one not so brave, you blew your horn continuously to attract attention until the robbers fled. If she, the 'blind' woman mentions to the cops that she was attacked on the east side, your entire story is going down the drain. In addition to having recommended props to add credibility to your story, you must have an airtight alibi, which you and your partner have at least vaguely rehearsed. Once you finish doing whatever it is you and the 'blind' person plan to do, get them the hell out of your home. If you want to go all the way with this 'blind' act, have the person emerge from your vehicle or taxi wearing the broken glasses or using the stick. This way you eradicate or at least alleviate the possibility of any of your nosy neighbors saying to your significant other at a later time, 'funny, I don't remember him or her going into your apartment with a walking stick.' Oh by the way this particular technique works better with women being the victim. Few men are going to believe that their frail little wives would leave the safety and comfort of their vehicles to risk their necks for another, especially a man. Make sure that when they leave, they get in a cab or they get into your vehicle but no matter what, make sure your significant other does not leave with you. Reason being, if your super sensitive, good Samaritan, significant other wants to guarantee that the 'attacked' individual makes it home safely and they have to continue with the 'blind' act, chances are John Q. Murphy (founder of Murphy's Law) will place some nosey, loquacious, smart Alec in front of the 'blind' person's residence just long enough for them to ask 'hey, what's with the disguise, Halloween party or something?' What will you do then? Remember two things; lying about someone is easy. Lying with someone is extremely the opposite. Also remember, this technique only helps before or after you do the do – never during. No further explanation should be necessary.

Watching the news, especially the traffic report is beneficial. Reason being, minor accidents are an almost daily occurrence in major cities. The one thing news reporters don't often do is show the people who were involved in the accident or show the vehicles involved unless it was a major accident on the highway or unless there were fatalities. This is beneficial to cheaters because if a cheater uses the 'honey, I had a fender bender' excuse, all you or the disbelieving spouse would have to do is turn on the news and if the newscaster mentions a delay due to an accident at the location the suspected spouse previously mentions, the cheater is home free. Of course then there is always the problem of vehicle damage. If you are the one cheating and you get your significant other to believe the story about you being involved in an accident, what will you say if they inspect the car for damage and find none? This is something only people who live apart need to worry about. If you live with the person you are cheating on, chances are you will be smart enough to rectify this problem before you get home – but if you are like those elusive happy couples who live apart from one another and you use this excuse, there is always the possibility of your partner garnering 'instant concern' for your well being and actually dropping everything to come over and make sure you are alright. To counteract this possibly negative situation, an easy solution would be to create an accident yourself – and this could be accomplished by driving into a fire hydrant or into a parking lot wall or highway guardrail. There are many places to have a backup 'accident' but the key to accomplishing this successfully is to have as few witnesses as possible. There is however always the problem of loving your car too much to see a scratch on her. I understand this totally because I am a car owner myself but if given the choice, I would most definitely rather have scratches and body damage on my car than on my person.

Another method, which helps shift focus from infidelity, is the usage of computers. People who are computer literate have some of the best excuses in the world because one can always have the person they're cheating with call and say they need help with their computer and that they're willing to pay. The reason this lie works so well is because computers are infamous for having problems or if not for having problems, then at least for being difficult to operate. The only potential downside to this is the problem of your significant other wanting to go with you to perform your repairs, especially if they're after normal business hours. What helps in this situation is the reverse psychology thing. Use the 'you don't trust me' line. Remind them that 'if there's no trust, there's no relationship.' Now chances are they may have every reason in the world not to trust your dirty, nasty, cheating ass but if you make them feel as if they are hurting you with the accusation, they will more than likely back off.

Timing is everything. When a person is being natural, few things are spontaneous. There is no 'hey let's go to the hotel and get our freak on' or 'I'm gonna drive down to my natural partner's job for a little nookie after lunch.' There must be availability on both sides as well as prior notification. This is often very difficult because part of the very definition of infidelity dictates sleeping with someone who is in a relationship. Therefore several precautions must be taken into account before any natural behavior is to take place. The first thing is location, location, location. I mentioned before that hotels were the ideal spots to perpetrate romantic liaisons. In my opinion, they are still the best options but not the only ones available. Close, single friends who live by themselves are often asked if their residence can be used as the alternate hotel. Hotel fees are sometimes outrageous, so a friend who has a nicely furnished one bedroom can do just fine. Once the place is secured, the dates must be agreed upon. Someone saying 'Tim, I need to borrow your place tomorrow night, I got this girl I wanna bang' is not proper notification because if the timing is okay for Tim and for his friend, it might not be okay for the female. Not to mention Tim may live in an area close to where someone who this particular woman knows may reside. All three need to be in agreement. The accepted rule of thumb is a one-week notification period, meaning if there is this type of debauchery scheduled, everybody should be in agreement as to the place and time at least one week in advance. There should also be in place an alternate location as well as a rain date. Let's say Tim gets sick during the seven-day waiting period and needs to be hospitalized. His friend will no doubt be concerned but that concern will more than likely be overshadowed by the concern he has for the female he was supposed to boink in Tim's house. Before the place is secured, there must be a secure method of contacting each person involved. People think this part is easy but this is where the majority of the mistakes are made. What many people who are either contemplating or planning an affair will do is call and divulge pertinent and damaging information from their homes, not realizing that THE WALLS HAVE EARS. The ears can be in the form of children, phone records or through an actual listening device planted to catch this very type of indiscretion. People don't realize that if requested, some cell and home phone companies will send an itemized list of charges; meaning which phone numbers were dialed and which were received from a particular number. This can be at the request of the phone owner or it can be an included feature of the phone service. When there are repeated calls to or from a particular number, suspicion will be raised. People also don't realize that children, especially young ones are the equivalent of elongated sponges – meaning they soak up everything they hear. Children don't know what discretion means. They will tell anything, no matter how damaging – all while thinking its funny or the right thing to do. Some people who suspect infidelity will go so far as to purchase a recording device, which can be activated from across town and strategically plant it in certain parts of the home. Some phones have such a feature, which when activated will allow the caller to listen to the immediate area in which the phone is placed. To counteract this, a person must never allow himself or herself to get caught up. He or she must call from a payphone when talking to the natural partner. If the cheating couple is too technologically advanced or sterile to stand around and use the public payphones, they can always purchase two prepaid phones to only be used when talking to one another. The brain must be the notepad because writing something on a piece of paper brings about the possibility for that piece of paper to get lost and found by the person the cheater would least like it to.

After securing the appointment and the place, the next necessary precaution is mode of travel, followed by the 'cover your ass' lie. The mode of travel is the most overlooked because many people feel that when they are doing wrong, they themselves are the only ones who see them. They don't realize that people can look at a license plate one time and remember it or that they can remember what direction they saw a particular vehicle driving at and at what time. When considering mode of travel, either have a taxi service or have a same sex associate drive you to the particular location. In the case above with Tim, the best thing for his friend would be to have Tim pick him up and drive to Tim's house or he and Tim use public transportation to get to Tim's house. Once there, Tim's friend can call the woman and have her come over or Tim can go back out and pick her up, then bring her back to his house. This is both, good and bad. Good because everybody, including Tim's friends' significant other, who observes Tim's female friend will also observe Tim in close proximity. This is bad because Tim's friends' significant other can, if she knows where Tim lives, always stop by. Some of you may be wondering why would the significant other stop by the home of the husband's best friend and the answer is simple. Whenever the suspicion level about infidelity is raised, a person will rarely play detective on their own. They will ask for help. And since the majority of the time, the best friend knows about what's going on in the relationship before the significant other, the best friend will be the first stop.

If a couple lives apart, and there are questions about fidelity in the relationship, the suspecting party can always 'mail' a letter to the home of the suspected party to make them drop their defenses. This is or can be accomplished with the assistance of the 'brave and foolish' individuals who use the home to cheat. Many people have either the type of jobs, which require them to take trips out of town or relatives who live too far away for a weekly visit. If the traveling party is the one who has doubt about the relationship, he or she can always 'pretend' to go away or actually go away and come home early. What this person can also do is address and stamp a letter to the significant other, from the place they are believed to be. What he or she can do then is wait for the mail person who delivers the mail to the significant others address and then ask very nicely if he or she will place the sent letter inside the box. If the mail person has reservations, the story of 'I know he or she is cheating on me because they think I'm out of town. If they receive a letter from me, they will be convinced that I am still out of town so it's a good chance they will bring the person they're cheating with to the house' can be used. If the mail person has been in a similar situation, chances are he or she may sympathize and place the letter in the box. Once the suspected significant other receives the out of town letter, he or she will more than likely be placed into a false sense of security, which may allow or prompt them into bringing the natural partner home. There are several possible red flags with this plan, for instance there is a metered stamp, which goes over the stamp, which is bought by the sender once a letter leaves the post office. If the significant other is observant, they may notice or check for this. What may counter this, is the fact that the letter is from the significant other - meaning the suspected cheater may be so enthused that the other partner is sending a letter from where ever, they may not check any other part of the envelope. If a person would like to go a little further with this, they can always go to a stationary store and pick up a stamp themselves. The stamp does not have to precisely match those in the post office because as long as not too much pressure is applied to the envelope, the barely legible, inked lines should suffice. There is also the possibility that the mail person will say no. This can be countered by either leaving the envelope on the floor or the table or anywhere in the general vicinity of the mailbox. (Right here sounds about right for a disclaimer) Just for the record, I am not advising anyone to go out and mess with the U.S. postal service – I am just making up examples as I go along because I know and you know that the information contained within this publication is for academic study only, right? Some people in this world are so brazen that they will cheat whenever the significant other is away from the home or too far away to get back in time to catch them. If the above method is employed, a potential or actual cheater may think 'I've got free range to do whatever because my significant other is wherever.' While the suspected party is delusional with that belief, the suspecting partner can stake out the suspected residence for adulterous activity. Often times a person only has a cellular phone as means of contact. This is good because a person can be almost anywhere and make or receive a call. This is bad because of the exact same reason. A person can live in New York but tell you they're in Ohio on business. If they know someone in Ohio, they can contract that person to answer their phone by saying you are either working in the field or just generally unavailable. If a person cannot reach their significant other by any way except their cell phone and they happen to receive a letter from the significant other, addressed from out of state, they will be more likely to believe that's where the significant other is. The bad part about many people's activities is that they will only monitor them when they think they themselves are being monitored. Ever notice how cameras in the workplace cut down immensely on theft? Employing the above method is the same as an employer using spy cameras to covertly watch the activities of his employees. You will get to see what goes on when a person thinks they are not being watched.

The final precaution necessary is the 'cover your ass' or 'back up' lie. These lies are not usually told by the cheater but by the cheaters' close associates who know and have agreed to be part of the deception. The cover your ass or back up lie is one which resembles 'I just saw your husband or wife getting on the train' or 'your significant other left his or her phone at my house by mistake.' These lies are put in place just in case there is ever need for a second alternate location. For instance, let's say Tim's wife came home early from her business trip in Seattle and wanted to spend time alone with her husband. All the previous planning would go down the drain, unless the couple had a second alternate location. If they did, the cover your ass lie would fit just perfectly because the cheater would already know what to say whenever they got home so as not to contradict the person who told the cover your ass lie to the significant other. Using the two above lies, if Tim's friend had to go somewhere else to boink his natural partner, the story about him leaving his phone would be just the thing to by him some time. Someone saying 'I just saw your husband or wife getting on the train' would also by time as well as provide confirmation when that person reaches home with the same story.

Chapter Three
How Many Times Can A Person Be In Love?

For years people have had this belief that love – true love, only comes around once in a lifetime. There is a continued belief that when a person finds the 'one' everything in life will be just peachy. No problem will be too great and if there ever was a problem, which seemed insurmountable, together a couple would always possess the necessary tools to overcome. The answer to a question such as this is, for lack of a better word, tricky. Tricky because there are many different types of love as well as many different types of things and people to be in love with. Women love shoes. Parents love their children. Men and women love one another. All three of the previous examples are types of love but they are not exclusive. Ask any woman about her footwear and I'm willing to bet that ninety nine percent of them who have the resources to afford more than one pair will have more than one pair. And I do not believe it's due to fashion or employment restrictions as much as it is the basic desire to have more than one. I'm also willing to bet that almost all of those women will have one special pair they love over all others. There are many families today that have more than one child. Some of these people will wait two years before they have their second child, some wait longer and a few only wait until the recommended month and a half before they start trying again. What many of these people do after having their first child is show an unsurpassed level of love and attention to that child - a level, which transcends into the next child and future children. I believe it to be unfathomable that a parent can love one child above the other. I can understand a parent being excluded from a child's life and that parent's fondness for that child growing more than say a child who is in the home with that parent but I believe love reinvents itself each time a child is born. There's a question, which people have been asking but no one has been able to answer except parents who are mad at their kids and that is 'if you have two kids and they are both in danger of dying and you could only save one, which one would you go for? What some ignorant people would do is say whomever your choice would be the one you supposedly love more. More is not an adequate word, which should be used when talking about love between children. Different is acceptable because most parents love their children for different reasons, the most important and most shared reason I believe is because the children are a part of them. There is no way I can understand a parent loving one child above the other. It is possible to love the things that one may do more than the other but the actual being; the unconditional love cannot be separated. Men and women fall in and out of love like they fall in and out of bed. Is this real love? Who knows? There is this soul mate belief, where one perfect person is supposed to be out there for you and only you. I always wondered is there one person whom you can be totally and unequivocally in love with and they can share that feeling or is it just that two people get tired of looking and decide to make this relationship work at all costs. There are several factors, which drive a person toward another. There are some things a person may 'love' about another and other things that person may love about someone else. Love is having a person who fulfills you. Love is having a person who will do for you and your family. Love is a union where two people strive to keep the relationship going. Love is 50/50. Love is unconditional. If the saying, there's one perfect person for everyone actually had any merit, the only reason I could see for there being there being a few billion people on earth would be for people to 'try before they buy' so to speak. I never try to advocate promiscuity or infidelity but think about the word billion. I am not going to use census type statistics to get an exact number of people who are presently residing on this earth but let's just use that number. A billion is a lot of anything, let alone people. If you started meeting people from the day you were born and continued meeting them from sun up until sun down until the day you died, assuming you lived to be one hundred, chances are you would never meet them all. If a person met just one person of the opposite sex and remained with that person for life, that person would be doing himself or herself a serious disservice when it comes to options. Love can happen more than once. Who's to say what level of love governs your existence? If you love someone because they treat you the best you've ever been treated and several years later you meet someone who treats you better, what is there stopping you from falling in love again? A person can be in love everyday of their life and each day with something totally different. I know of many people that fall in love with the newest rap stars or the newest singers or even the newest supermodels and this happens all the time. But is this real love? Or course it's not. This normally would not be any type of problem but what people sometimes have difficulty with is distinguishing this type of love or 'infatuation' from real love. Now I like to believe that everybody in this world knows what infatuation is, even if they don't like to admit it. Infatuation consists of things like shoes – and we all know how much women love their shoes. This is not real love nor can it be confused with real love because real loves requires things like commitment, loyalty and honesty – you know, the usual suspects. A person cannot apply these things toward inanimate objects like shoes although many women do throw the word around quite often don't they? People also throw around the word love when they meet somebody and establish a connection, as in 'I met this guy and I think I'm in love!' Again, it is close to impossible to meet a person and instantly fall in love with that person without knowing anything about said person. It is very possible to meet someone and say 'I know he or she is the one for me' and then after a period of courtship and togetherness, have feelings solidify and actually fall in love but to just say it and then have it happen, I believe a person would have better luck at winning the Powerball lottery. I do not believe there is any textbook time frame or limit on love or on how long it can last or how many times an individual can actually be in love because besides everybody in this world being different and having a different protocol regarding his or her relationships, some people do not have any conceptual idea of what real love actually is. People love to listen to best friends, family members and television shows to get a better understanding of what love actually entails. This is good on the one hand because many television shows are often based on true life experience and family members and friends often have different love experiences which they can share and possibly help another. This is bad on the other hand because what if the television show, that an individual decides to base his or her love life after shows that infidelity is an acceptable option for problems in the relationship? What if one of the relationships that a friend or family member has just happens to be an abusive one? Will the individual following this behavior know that is wrong and immediately stop or will they continue to follow because they look up to family and friends and figure that since family and friends are so smart, whatever these people are doing must be right? The problem with a lot of people in this world is that they love to learn but they hate to be taught. When professional people like the clergy or those that actually specialize in relationships offer advice, many people in this world run from that advice. But just let that advice be given by someone that has little to no conceptual idea of how to keep a relationship going and all of a sudden people wanna listen. Until there is a worldwide understanding of what love actually is, there will continue to be different interpretations of love and different interpretations of the word relationship. Now the last thing I want to do is turn this into a religious lesson but if people would maybe pop into a church maybe once or twice and get an understanding of what an actual commitment in the eyes of a higher power actually means, there would be a more complete understanding of what love is. There would not be all of this infidelity. There would not be all of this disease and killing due to broken commitments. Most importantly there would be an answer for the chapter question, how many times can a person be in love?

Chapter Four
What Drives A Man To Cheat?

Since the publication of The Correct Way To Fool Around part one, everybody and their mother has bombarded me with inquisitions about the specifics on why men cheat. It seems the explanation previously given about every man possibly having a different reason for infidelity was not sufficient enough. They wanted detailed information. Now to sequentially list every reason or even half of all the reasons behind why men cheat would be, to say the least, impossible - Impossible because when it comes to why, I have found that some men seem to cheat for no reason, some men cheat for frivolous reasons, some men cheat for mental reasons and some men cheat for reasons beyond human comprehension. Before we get all into what drives a man to cheat, we should examine a couple of the differences between the beliefs about men and women.

The Double Standard – This is the widely held belief mainly by men but shared by many women that when it comes to sex, men can 'fool around' until their hearts content without repercussion or label, except for the ever popular 'he's just being a man.' This belief goes on to say that it is expected for men to be less faithful than woman. According to the double standard, men will always be viewed as praise – getters for promiscuity, whereas women will continue to be harlots, jezebels and straight up sluts, hence the expression 'a man's fame is a woman's shame.' When a woman has the same number or even half the number of 'relationships' as that of a promiscuous man, she is labeled everything from 'fast' to the 'whore of Babylon.' People do not be disillusioned. This belief will not change. Just as there are race restrictions from birth, there are also ones relating to gender. A man's fame will always be a woman's shame because in relationships, few are actually viewed as equals. In most relationships, sexual or otherwise, a man is almost always seen as the conqueror and the woman is almost seen as the one being conquered. This long-standing belief stems from the idea of women being eternally maternal and men being perpetual playboys. 'No man has or can have a positive reputation for being a motherly type of parent without ridicule. Women on the other hand cannot enjoy the type or level of promiscuity that men are known to have without exceptionally derogatory labels.'

Friends – Another big belief about men & women is the one, which states women can be friends with men on a platonic level but men cannot be friends with women on the same. This belief stems from the double standard as well as the fallacy that women are so supposedly trustworthy and men are so supposedly not. 'Men are desire driven and women are emotionally charged.' That is the big belief, which may contribute to why the thought exists that both sexes cannot be friends. Man will always desire the woman and women will always desire an emotional commitment from the man.

Jabberwocky! For the longest time, men have been mistakenly described as the species without emotion. Men have emotion, I like to believe the same level of emotion as women – only men are not allowed to express them due to many of society's unwritten laws. As stated elsewhere in this chapter, there are women who act the same way men do but again, thanks to society, that type of acting must be kept under wraps. For those of you having trouble understanding facts and figures, let me explain. Everything in this world, I believe has a partner – an equal if you will. For every crazy, one-sided conversation having individual walking the streets, somewhere in this world, there is someone who loves or is looking to love them. For every wrong, there is an eventual retribution. For every man who desires only the physical aspects of a woman, there is one who desires everything else. And for every woman who is on this emotional kick, I believe that there are just that many who would like nothing more than to get her boots knocked every so often.

Reasons – some men are instilled with the belief that their sole vocation in life is to have as much sex as humanly possible. This belief can come from friends, especially in junior high and in high school or it can come from male role models, such as parents, older cousins or uncles. This belief can also come from the preponderance of sexual innuendo filled commercials, movies and music videos.

When young children grow up with unchallenged beliefs, very often, they tend to assume that whatever they absorb is true. Upbringing has always and will always be a major factor in how people turn out as adults. If a child is taught that it's okay to disrespect and dominate woman, it will be extremely hard for that child who becomes a grownup to be anything other than disrespectful and dominating later in life. The first thing people do when they encounter a racist or someone who exudes racist tendencies, other than say 'that's a sorry motherfucker' is speculate on what may have caused him or her to be that way and almost nine times out of ten the speculation ends up being 'he or she probably got it from his or her parents.' Yet when it comes to infidelity, people want to give every possible cause except that. They want to believe that infidelity is caused by not going to church enough or caused by watching too many x-rated movies. These two examples are not as preposterous as some may believe them to be. Church helps with many aspects of a person's life and with the strong support system many places of worship provide, it can be assumed that if a regular churchgoer was to miss a few Sundays, they might be more inclined to try what they might otherwise not. I'm not saying that if a person were to miss church today, he or she would go out and kill somebody tomorrow; I'm just saying that there are influences – negative and positive, all around us – all the time. The more a person is exposed to one type of influence, the less they will be influenced by the other – and vice versa. X-rated movies and porn in general have far too often gotten the blame for men cheating on their wives and significant others. The creation of the adult video I believe was to add excitement to otherwise dull and uneventful sexual encounters. By themselves, I doubt if a video or DVD can lead to unfaithfulness but what they can do is begin a person on the path to thinking about infidelity, especially if that is the type of movie they view. Once a person has the thought, other factors may follow, which can help make the transition from completely honest person to 'lying sack of shit' possible. Now while I don't believe videos and other types of porn can turn someone from honest to not, it must be stated that if a person was promiscuous or even moderately sexually active, the introduction of certain types of porn may trigger memories of enjoyable times that person may have had. It would then be up to that individual to decide if he or she wants to act on those desires or not. This reminds me of the argument people have been having for years about whether or not rap music has the capability to incite violence. Again, by itself I believe no. A person must be the type of individual who either already has a violent temper or who must be under the 'subliminal influences' some people believe are stored in the music. The type of music one listens to may help trigger an unpleasant memory or activate an impulse but I doubt seriously if listening to gangster rap will cause somebody to commit murder. When a person is born, they know nothing. They must be nurtured, loved and taught. A racist cannot be formed if no one teaches him to be that way. The same thing holds true for those who commit infidelity. They have to learn it from somewhere. As stated above, one of the biggest influences in a person's life is that person's parents or caretakers. These are the people who spend huge amounts of time either raising a child to be a productive member of society or a menace to society. Most of the people in this world I like to believe will raise their children to follow rules and do what rest of the world expects of them. But there are those who feel that there's nothing more important than having as much sex with as many women as they possibly can and also feel that that is how they should raise their sons. Is this right? Of course not but unfortunately other than making sure a child is fed, educated and generally taken care of, there is little one can say about the lessons one is taught in the home. So when a man commits infidelity, it is quite possible that he may have had strong influences from his very own family, which could have led up to his decision to cheat on his significant other. This is not to say that this is the only reason a man will cheat but this can definitely be a factor.

'Honey, the kids need shoes.' 'Honey, the cable bill is due.' 'Honey, you don't pick up after yourself.' 'Honey, you never cook.' 'Honey, you don't ever take me anywhere.' Sound familiar? Statements such as these, although often true, are what cause uneasiness in many relationships. More commonly known as nagging, this type of badgering, instead of helping a relationship will cause the party on the receiving end to go looking for stress relief – and as we all know stress relief usually comes in three forms. The first is separation from the anxiety, the second is alcohol or drug abuse to temporarily escape the problems caused by the anxiety and the third is a member of the opposite sex or same sex depending upon one's lifestyle. To be completely correct with this, it should be stated that nagging is almost never the sole and total cause for infidelity. A woman can nag a man until her lips fall off from exertion. If it doesn't bother that particular man too much, he will either ignore it or deal with it. Nagging leads to stress on the part of some men. That stress leads to headaches. Headaches lead to the mental dispute of do I really love this person or do I really need this shit? That mental dispute is another way of saying frustration. Sex with someone else then becomes an outlet for frustration. There are often other underlying factors, which lead to infidelity. These factors can be anything from a-z but what people will do is disguise the factors or rearrange them so that it will seem to the other person that those actual problems, causing all of the drama are small or non-existent.

One of the reasons a man will cheat is because the woman he is involved with is not 'what he really desires.' Some people think that this is a cheesy excuse but no one ever said reasons have to be well thought out and feasible to be valid. Contrary to popular belief, men don't only want sex when they involve themselves with the opposite sex. Men desire the same thing women do; someone to make them happy, someone to make them comfortable, and someone to make them feel a way in which no other can. Many people realize that you cannot always find this in one person but there are others who believe that what one lacks, another will have an abundance of. And so the search begins. The saying 'women fake orgasms, men fake relationships' is a general statement, which applies to many, many relationships today. Using the above example, a man will become involved with a woman for a multitude of reasons. Everything from 'she looks good' to 'she's got a good job' to she's got a great ass.' And each reason in his mind will be all which is necessary to initiate or facilitate a relationship. However, these reasons will only provide temporary satisfaction. A relationship is based on many things. Quite often people do not take into account all of those things when weighing the options of a relationship, especially men. Many men will focus on something, for instance the size of a woman's body, which will tempt them into a relationship. If and when the size of that particular woman's body is no longer what the man desires, little else will be left to sustain that relationship. I don't believe a man initially sets out to cheat once involved in a relationship as much as I believe he thinks with a short term type of mindset. When you have no long term plan for your life, you consistently find yourself searching for things to provide fulfillment. People go from job to job just like they go from person to person. There are many who say men fake relationships but I think it's more they are not completely ready for those relationships and once they get in them, they don't always know how to get out. That's when the faking sets in. On that note, there are hundreds of thousands of women (maybe more) who sincerely believe that cheating in men is an uncontrollable attribute. These women think that because someone just happens to be born a man, they are mindless, sex driven drones, who do not possess the will power or capability to resist temptation when faced with the prospect of another naked woman. From my experience, this belief comes from women who have been hurt and it is totally understandable. However, all men do not cheat – let me say it again; all men do not cheat, just as all women do not cheat. What I find is that a lot of men will play their relationships they way their women do. If a woman is brutally honest in her day-to-day activities and interactions, often the men will be too. The men can be faithful but they do it on a case-by-case basis. If a woman gives off the signal that she's cheating or that she does not care about cheating on the part of her significant other, he may cheat and not because he has absolute proof (which I believe is one of the only acceptable reasons for cheating or separation) but because he has the suspicion, which she does not care about alleviating. Here's another example; if a person is fearful that their life is in danger, the natural reflex will be to protect oneself. This can happen in many different ways but the bottom line is that a person thinks something will happen or is happening and they are taking the appropriate or necessary precautions. If you ever watch a very young child as they are about to fall the first thing they do is put their hands up to protect themselves or rather brace for impact. This is not usually taught, this is instinctive. This is often what people do when they cheat. They are bracing for the impact that cheating will eventually have on their lives. They cheat before they have complete proof because they are unsure if their partners are. They cheat to protect their feelings. People love to hear that cheating, especially male cheating is due to some kind of far out medical condition, which can't be reversed. As comforting as that would be to the probably millions of women who have been cheated on, I don't think that will ever be the cause. Men cheat, have always cheated and probably will always continue to do so. The reasons why, vary. One must remember two things; many men know why they indulge in affairs, whether they admit it or not and (2) the reasons given for infidelity are not always the reasons why infidelity was committed. 'It didn't mean anything – the opportunity was there and we just took advantage.' This is a very popular example of excuses, which are used once a man is caught cheating. Now true as it may be, it may not be the complete and/or only reason the affair took place. When a person says it didn't mean anything, you must ask whom didn't it mean anything to, the man or the woman he was sleeping with? Obviously the indiscretion meant enough for him to risk his present relationship with you, so it meant something. It may have meant to him fulfilling a fantasy that jacking off no longer could or it could have meant to her thrill fucking a married man.

Another reason some men cheat is because they feel that the women they are involved with do not understand them. Understanding comes in different forms. Understanding can be acceptance of a person's shortcomings. It can also be realizing that the differences between the sexes are more than just anatomical. Men need more than for a woman to be a bedside partner. Women have to be able to provide emotional support, as well as physical support when necessary. The belief is that men do not have feelings. Men are always strong; men are always tough, men do not cry. For the most part the prior statements are true but at least once in every man's existence there will come a time when life will be too much to handle, when the alleviation of stress will require much more than a few rounds in the bedroom or a few shots of Grey Goose. There will come a time when a man needs that hug from his significant other or an attentive yet silent ear while he vents the pressures of his job and finances. Many women are taught that the societal roles in which they are born cannot be escaped. The belief is that these women are not supposed to cross the gender lines, meaning they cannot be tough. They must be demure and submissive at all times. If they see their male role model failing, they do not help, they accept the failure. They think 'just leave him alone, he'll get over it' instead of 'he's falling, let me find out what I can do to help.' The societal beliefs today are that men have the hard jobs because they are the only ones who can do them. When it comes to construction workers, most of them are men. When it comes to mechanics, again most of them are men. When it comes to combat soldiers in the military, men are the ones sent to war. What do women do? Secretary, babysitter, maids and homemakers. As of late, these jobs have become somewhat unisex positions. The only difference is how they are now labeled. Secretary, which used to be a strictly female occupation is now called administrative assistant. Babysitting, which used to be an all – teenage girl occupation is now respectably called childcare. Maids too, were at one time, a strictly woman based operation but now they have progressed to include housekeeping in their title as well as men. Homemakers will always be women. When it applies to a man, the operative will be unemployed. This is not a sexist theory; this is how many in relationships as well as society at large see individuals. The belief is that a man will never require help from his 'lesser half' and if he does, he is not a complete man. This is one of the reasons men are so ashamed or hesitant to take money from a woman. They'll do it but they won't let it be known. When a man feels that he does not have that support system, he will go looking for another system of support. And that system of support does not have to be ravishingly beautiful or even moderately attractive. All that needs to exist is a shared comfort level, which is another way of saying sex. Some women who catch their men in these types of indiscretions may wonder how could infidelity occur when the other woman is not nearly as attractive or as shapely as they themselves are. This is a prime example of some women not understanding what their man is in need of. A woman does not have to look good to make a man feel good. Sometimes infidelity is just about the desire to have sex with somebody new. Most times however, it's about much, much more. Honesty and communication will not always eradicate being natural but it will alleviate the hell out of it. If a couple can talk freely about whatever without fear of hurting each others feelings, infidelity will stand little chance.

'Men cheat because it's in our nature' says Brian 20, New York. 'Women cheat because they catch us but we do it because we can't help it.'

'Men cheat because they have no moral or spiritual backbone' Name withheld, New York.

'Because they're dogs – straight up dogs!' Says 19 yr. old Shakema from Brooklyn.

'When a man is faithful and his girl, all of a sudden wanna stop, (making love)
that's when he cheats. I'm not saying its right but a man got needs.' Jose, 22, from The Bronx.
'Because we can' Jim Brown, Con Ed employee – New York Age withheld.

Chapter Five
What Drives A Woman To Cheat?

We have but two teachers in this life, parents and life experience. Schoolteachers, professors, bad relationships as well as good all fall under the life experience category. These things are the determining factors in how we turn out and how we treat others. Parents teach us (in regard to relationships) that they are either to be preserved and respected or entered into and exited out of like hula-hoops. Life experiences, on the same note, teach us that relationships can be wonderful or unbelievably ugly. There has been a long-standing argument about the forces, which drive a man to cheat and the ones, which propel women. As history will show, men cheat for damn near any reason under the sun – and as much as I hate to admit it, women do not. There is actually a limit to what will make them stray. To be as accurate and politically correct as possible, I polled a number of women to find out their reasons for hitching a ride on the infidelity bandwagon. The results were not so much surprising as they were shocking. Some women believed that if a man had a small penis (not small meaning less than average but small meaning less than what it takes to make a woman achieve orgasm) that it was okay for them to screw around. 'It's kind of like medicinal marijuana' as stated by Elaine S, 31 of Manhattan. She continued 'it's not right or completely legal but it makes you feel so much better than conventional methods – and in the end, isn't feeling good what it's all about?'

Anita F, 40 of The Bronx disagrees saying retaliation is the only acceptable reason to ever break the solemn vow of matrimony or commitment. 'Two wrongs do not make a right but what is good for the goose is good for the gander.'

'Too many chances' is the reason given by Vivian L, 52 of New Windsor, Ct. 'If a man messes around and gets caught, if there is love, true love in the relationship, he deserves and should receive forgiveness. I mean for crying out loud, everybody makes mistakes – but if that man continues to fail to learn from his mistakes, then he should be on the receiving end. It's said that true love is everlasting but for that to actually exist, there must be mutual feeling on both sides. If a person in love continually gets badgered with heartbreak, the feeling will eventually subside - no matter how much love there was in the beginning. Sometimes a person has to experience how his or her actions actually affect the person they are involved with.'

Tamika 36 of The Bronx says 'women cheat because of lack of attention and because of the small pee pee syndrome.' She also considers weak men, those who present no challenge or control, a definite cause of straying. There used to be a widely held belief that women would only cheat when the relationship was basically over or because the woman's emotional needs were not being recognized or stimulated. But as stated above and just like with men, reasons, which drive woman to infidelity are often varied as well. The one reason I'd like to focus on is the small pee pee syndrome. Women have been embroiled in a major controversy about the size doesn't matter thing for many years now. It has been said that when a person loves another, many things, especially this can be overlooked. As of late however, more and more women are using the excuse that they are not being satisfied in the bedroom as reason to cheat. Men have been using this excuse about not being satisfied in the bedroom too but women seem to feel that it's more of an issue when it applies to them. A fair argument would be that once a person experiences an orgasm, they would desire to experience that feeling again and again. If they were to only experience that pleasure one time and then be subject to life with someone who could not provide them with that type of enjoyable experience, they would long for it and eventually go after it, I believe to keep their sanity. No matter where I go, it always seems that people undervalue the importance or impact that sex has in other people's lives. The desire for sex is powerful, sometimes overwhelmingly so. To have that desire suppressed, for any reason will only cause it to eventually resurface with tenfold fury. People kill because of sex. They even lie, rob and blackmail others to engage in it. Last but not least, they will leave the person to whom they have professed undying fidelity to if the sex is not up to par. When a feeling and that's all sex really is, can override a lifelong commitment, one has to ask themselves, which holds a higher place – the promise of fidelity or the orgasmic response? It's been said many times that women fake orgasms, men fake relationships. For a woman to deny herself that type of pleasure I believe that she must not enjoy sex or she's getting it somewhere else.

In my interviewing of several women for this topic, many of them have mentioned that they 'feel' when a man is being unfaithful. This of course intrigued me so I pressed the issue a little further and these women told me that some of them actually wake up during the night with the thought of infidelity on their minds. Some tell me that they have had very descriptive dreams of the infidelity act. They have mentioned that not only could they envision the circumstances surrounding the affair, they could also feel physical sensations. Now of course as a man I have no way of knowing if these women were lying, were that much in love or were actually speaking from past experience but for one thing, their arguments were strong enough to at least convince themselves.

Now out of all of the reasons I was given for women partaking in the act of infidelity, I think the biggest one outside of revenge was the reason of the man never being at home. The women I had spoken with were all in agreement with this one. They stated that 'men are allowed to have their time away from us just as we should have our time away from them but when it becomes excessive that's when our minds start to wonder.' I asked does that lead to cheating by itself and most of them were in agreement again when they said no. It turned out to be a number of things, with the culmination being not enough time being spent with the wife and family. By itself, these women stated spending time away from the family would not normally cause any woman to go and cheat. But the constant harassment by single suitors and even the male whores who never see my man and I together, made me start to wonder 'what was he doing while he was away so much?' 'Was he doing the same thing to some other women that these guys are trying to do to me?' In addition to that, there was the fact that he and I were having some relationship problems, which were not resolved or not getting resolved and he wants to start staying out all night? The more I spoke with these women, the more I began to realize that the reason many of them gave for cheating (those that did and those that knew of someone that did) was due mainly to the communication breakdown. These women almost unanimously agreed that once they and their significant others stopped speaking to one another, things went pretty much down hill from there. Once the communication was gone, the suspicion set in and once the suspicion set in, the trust set out.

Many of these women had based their infidelity not on the significant others infidelity but on the infidelity of the significant other of the woman's best friend. They said 'yeah, if your man doing it, my man probably doing it too.' These women would be going through something in their relationship and their girlfriends would be going through something in their relationship as well and if infidelity just happened to occur in the relationship of the girlfriend, then the other would believe that infidelity was going on in hers as well – even if there was no proof to substantiate that belief. And because this belief is introduced, some of these women would use that belief as reason to initiate an affair of their own. They called it protecting their hearts. This taught me something. A lot of infidelity is based on the belief of infidelity – even though infidelity may or may not have happened. Many of these women who admitted cheating said that there were other issues in the relationship, which worked in conjunction with the man staying out all the time but the fact that the issues were never worked on is what definitely led to the ultimate decision to stray.

Chapter Six
The Psycho Factor

Deception, lies and hidden agendas – These are the ingredients, which make up what many like to call 'The Psycho Factor.' The Psycho Factor is the reason members of one gender deem the others as crazy or mentally unstable. Historically, deception has been used to trick people into doing any and everything they were not intent on doing or not aware of themselves actually doing. Deception has been used to sell cars, have sex and even get certain elected officials into office. (Can anybody say Florida?) The basic rule behind deception is if you make something so appealing and believable, whether it's true or not, people will find interest. It's the theory behind fool's gold; push up bras and many relationships. The thing about deception, which many seem to constantly overlook, is the fact that it can work two ways, the initial deception and reverse deception from the part of the other partner. An example of this is Kim is married to Ryan. Ryan is secretly cheating on Kim With Tasha. Kim is secretly bisexual and cheating on Ryan with Tasha also. Triple deception is neither Ryan nor Kim being aware that Tasha is secretly sleeping with somebody else. There is an overly used but rarely heeded saying, which reads if something looks too good to be true, it probably is. A brand new 2009 Chevy Impala selling for $1000 is an unbelievable deal which would probably only be available to family members, businesses going out of business or people who have lost their damned minds. What is not too commonly known is that aside from all of the previous examples, the car could have been in New Orleans at the time of hurricane Katrina and could have sustained tremendous interior damage, which is not visible to the naked or inexperienced eye. A person may be deceived into buying this car because it seems too good to be true and no one wants to miss out on the deal of a lifetime. Lies are self-explanatory. They are a form of deception, which usually or most often are not of the positive kind. Lies are bad but sometimes they are able to be overlooked and many times even forgiven. An example of a lie which can be forgiven (like people actually need instruction) is telling someone you care about that his or her steadily increasing weight does not bother you when it actually repulses you. An example of a lie, which is not as easily forgivable, is 'I know who kidnapped your child but I told you I didn't because they are friends of mine.' Hidden agendas are another reason people can become part of the psycho factor. A hidden agenda is what I described in my second book, Relationships, pacification for crazy people, as the three-month façade. People who have hidden agendas get into relationships for every reason except honesty. They desire something that their partner has or is able to acquire. Most people in relationships are in relationships for that exact same reason, they want something from the other person – only difference most people in relationships will not hide the fact that they want something. Most people in relationships will let the other person know that they are looking for commitment or stability or whatever it is they are in fact looking for. The fact that people have to resort to trickery to procure or maintain a relationship is reason enough to doubt their integrity as well as sanity. These people who deceive, lie and have hidden agendas, basically have a pre set plan for their lives. They know that many of the people they are potentially interested in will not be interested in that plan so they have to do what's necessary to get and keep them in a relationship. When the people who fall victim to the deceit, lies and hidden agendas wake up and realize 'hey, this is not what I signed on for' and then try to leave, the psycho factor sets in and the ones perpetrating the deceit begin to show their true, crazy ass colors. Here's a popular for instance: a man is married with kids, lives with his wife and family and by all outside accounts is happy. One of his co-workers garners an attraction to him even though she knows he is potentially unavailable. They begin conversations about infidelity and continue with hypothetical scenarios about what would happen before, during and after the 'dirty deed.' The understanding is in place that if anything were to ever happen, it would just be a physical liaison and nothing else. Both parties eventually agree and commit the indiscretion. Soon after, the female co-worker begins to call 'just to say hi.' That's not really so bad because letting someone know that you value them as more than just a sex toy is always comforting but what happens after that, which is potentially detrimental, is the holiday and special event gift giving. It starts with a card or a sweater at Christmas but then zooms to no holiday can pass by without them giving you something. This is when the female employee catapults herself from the 'friend's with benefits' zone into the 'one sided boyfriend and girlfriend' zone. This zone is one sided because the 'boyfriend' has no idea that he has been bestowed with that honor. The female employee buys expensive gifts for the married co-worker but gets nothing in return, except sex. The female continues to provide financial assistance and gifts in return for sexual favors in the hopes that the male will eventually leave his wife and or family. The woman even goes so far as to tell her friends that the man is more a part of that relationship than he actually is. When the married man does not leave his wife and family and the female employee slowly comes to the realization that she was nothing more than weekend stimulation, she begins to act nuts. She threatens to inform the wife, among other things and just generally begins to act psycho. The psycho-ness continues to the point of phone calls all hours of the night, unscheduled visits, even threats to assassinate the male's character as well as his person. Police involvement is not too far behind because either you will find yourself filing an order of protection against her crazy ass or she will lie and try to have you arrested – if she can get at you no other way. Some of these 'psycho' people are living in their own little fantasy world where they believe that if they act as though the person they attach themselves to are actually in a relationship, then magically a relationship will form. When it doesn't form, these people flip out and that's when all the drama begins. The bad part about these types of situations is that they are easily avoidable and preventable. To do this, always be upfront with a partner or prospective partner. Tell them, over and over if need be, where the relationship is going and or where you want it to go. Be brutally freaking honest if you have to. If both parties conform to this rule, there will never be any misunderstandings or if there are instances of misunderstandings, they will be very few. The nicest people in the world can become the most evil if their feelings are riled the wrong way. Damn the saying about a woman scorned. If a psycho has to deal with hurt feelings caused by you, male or female, you will have to consistently watch your back – as well as the backs of your family. People who have issues or 'hidden agendas' are more dangerous than regular folks who just happen to get involved with the wrong person because when a person has issues, nine times out of ten those issues are problems, which are directly related to that person's emotional well being. A person who has unresolved issues, whether they are due to a prior relationship or due to family upbringing will make the life of the person they get involved with absolute hell if the relationship is not going the way they want. The problem with these deceptive, issue having, true agenda hiding people is that it's almost impossible to just look at them and tell which ones will turn out with a few problems and which ones will actually be a part of the psycho factor. Getting involved in a relationship with someone who is part of the psycho factor is bad enough but it completely pales in comparison to already being in a committed relationship with someone, then cheating with someone who keeps his or her true agendas hidden. (Aka the psycho factor.) A person can be thinking 'hey I'm just gonna cheat on my husband or wife, maybe once or twice, get it outta my system, then go back to my relationship as if nothing out of the ordinary has happened and with possibly a new outlook on the relationship's future.' Unfortunately, most times the situation is a little different on the side of the person who was recruited for sex. This person could be thinking 'I have found the man or woman of my dreams' 'This person loves me' or 'This person is going to leave his wife or her husband for me.' This causes massive problems! This causes confusion beyond repair where the heart is concerned. You see, sometimes, in fact many times when a person's emotions are stimulated, there is little room for logical thought. Logical thought dictates that a person should get to know whoever it is he or she feels attracted to before giving up the drawers. However, when a person is in lust, which is most often confused with early stages of love, that person will do everything he or she can to keep the relationship going for as long and as happy as possible. This includes catering to his or her every whim, having sex all the time (even when a person does not want to) and acting contradictory to how one would normally act if there were no feelings of interest at all. The reason this is so bad is because some people in this world are fucking heartless. Sorry but there's no other politically correct way to say it. People will lead you on, they will let you empty out your bank accounts on them, they will even completely screw up your otherwise good credit – and while you are catching feelings, hoping that this special person for whom you are doing all of this crazy shit appreciates at least an iota of a portion of it, this person is at home with the husband or wife, not giving your existence on this planet a single solitary fucking thought. This, right here is what causes a person to go get a pistol and shoot the life out of someone. Now by no means of any stretch of the imagination am I saying this is right but when a person does everything their heart and soul and upbringing tells them is right and expected in a relationship and the other party basically bitch smacks this person's efforts right up side the head, employing the above method of revenge could be understood. Again, I am the last person to condone violence but people must remember, sometimes their actions can drive another fucking crazy. In other words, what you do that you think is commonplace, could be propelling the other straight into the psycho factor. Verbal communication is essential to counteract present issues and future problems. Folks always say that quiet people are often crazy and not because you have to be quiet to be crazy but because there is no outlet for their frustrations. Quiet people are not crazy; they just have different outlets for their frustrations. Many times these outlets just happen to be guns and chainsaws and shit like that. Just think how different quiet people would be if they only communicated more with not only their partners but people in general. In the example above, where one party does everything and the other completely takes him or her for granted, the main thing missing, which allowed that type of treatment to go on was little more than a lack of communication. People have to communicate from day one and even before day one to alleviate the possibility of potential problems down the road. Far too often couples break up and say 'if only I had known he was gonna turn out like that' or 'if only I had known she was the type to...' Instead of people rushing to judgment and ending up having a bunch of 'if only's' or a bunch of regrets, how about preventing these problems beforehand? The easiest way again is by talking. Talk about what type of relationship you want. Talk about what kind of marriage you want. People should even talk about what kind of sexual escapade they want or are expecting. When people communicate effectively, there is little room for error. Each party knows what is expected. When people assume they know what the other party desires or when they know what the other party desires and it is not what they themselves want but they go along with it anyway just to satisfy their own lusty or greedy desires, there will be trouble. There will be misunderstandings, there will be heartaches, but most importantly there will be a path leading straight into the psycho factor.

Chapter Seven
Acceptable Excuses For Infidelity

There are none! Next chapter. Okay, just joking. When it comes to infidelity, few things in this world other than someone's incapacitation merit forgiveness. The very idea of someone breaking a vow so solemn can evoke little more than feelings of extreme hatred and pain. Mistakes are often forgivable but the reasons the mistakes were made in the first place are what truly require focus. When caught in a transgression, many people will say they were unaware of what they were doing at the time, sort of like temporary insanity. This is a very popular and accepted excuse, especially in the legal world – even if it is bullshit. To my understanding, temporary insanity is little more than a person having full knowledge and conscience of his or her actions but not having the willpower to control them. That person, combined with their legal representative will then devise a strategy to the effect of 'I blacked out and during the time I blacked out, I had no conceptual idea of what I was doing – therefore I should not be held accountable.' People who commit infidelity make conscious decisions, maybe not well thought out decisions but conscious decisions nonetheless. For someone to say that they got together with a person of the opposite sex, removed each other's clothes, engaged in physical relations with that person – while they were already in a relationship and not know it was wrong or to say they were unaware of their actions is total and utter bullshit. It hovers somewhere near the same level of bullshit as the individual who takes an automatic weapon, kills thirty or forty people, then attempts to convince the judicial system, as well as society at large that he or she is crazy. What's crazy is the judicial system, which lets that type of individual get away with that type of activity – just like the people who accept the excuse 'I didn't know what I was doing' when it comes to infidelity. Everybody knows the actions they make. Someone punches another in the mouth, it's a pretty safe bet they are fully aware of what they have done. What is not always known are driving forces behind or the repercussions of those actions. That punch in the mouth could have come about because one person may have spoken rudely about another's mother or wife. That punch in the mouth could also cause the one who got punched to procure a pistol, seek out the individual who punched him or her and shoot the life out of the other. There are some excuses regarding infidelity, which if are not completely legitimate, are somewhat acceptable. One of those 'acceptable' excuses is the one about cheating because a person's significant other withholds intimacies from their partner. This is what one can call a borderline excuse because while it may not be completely accepted by everyone, it can be very well understood. The act of sex has been known to be overwhelmingly powerful. It is something a person must either never indulge in or indulge in on a continual basis. If a person never indulges in certain intimacies, it will be impossible for that person to miss them. If however someone is exposed to something they enjoy and garner an instant attraction to, to, on a later occasion, stop or restrict that something, will naturally create a longing and possibly an unquenchable thirst for it. In most committed relationships, there is a small amount of leeway regarding the trust issue because the amount of fidelity shared is only as strong as people's morals. But in marriage, withholding intimacies, especially when both partners know that they are unable to just get up and go 'get some' when their significant other is not acting right, borders on cruel and unusual punishment. For the most part, women will accept or understand this excuse because they know that other women are historically the 'major withholders' in many relationships.

The women who accept or understand this withholding excuse are sympathetic to the man's predicament and while they may not be big supporters of genuine infidelity, many of them are genuine supporters of what's fair.

The best 'acceptable' reason for infidelity is the one everybody tries to avoid and this one is the 'I cheated on you because I don't love you.' I know there are some sensitive people reading this right now who are probably saying 'if they don't love each other, then why are they together?' and the best answer I can provide is because they need each other for reasons other than sex. Some of those reasons may include kids or may be because one of the members in that relationship has a lot more money than the other. It should be known and understood that dependency is always a reason when it comes to relationships. A person who has nowhere else to go may get involved with someone he or she does not really love if that person has ample room to spare. A person who does not have a job will quite often become involved with someone who has steady employment, as well as steadily increasing back accounts. Now this is not to say that in every relationship one individual is constantly taking advantage of the other. This is to say that in all relationships, the parties involved are dependent upon one another – and as in the examples above; some more than others. People in this world fall in and out of love all the time. What too, too many of them do however is continue in a relationship when there is really no real reason to continue. And one of the reasons why is because they are often scared of truth; truth being, I don't love you anymore or at all. People all too often think that all relationships will eventually fizzle out after a while – and to an extent this is true. Very few relationships can continue with the momentum, which was present at the beginning without consistent efforts at improvement. But while some relationships slow down, others just stop. People need to know which is which. For those which have stopped, meaning there is nothing left resembling excitement, communication or commitment – cheating often becomes a viable option and 'reasonable' excuse. There will always be those who will say that allowing infidelity to enter into a committed relationship is wrong no matter the circumstances but those people must be able to say that they have walked a mile in the moccasins of the particularly troubled couple. Nobody really knows what other people and other couples endure. All people really know is what they see as well as what those particular and troubled people tell them. And as most people know or should know, what you see isn't always all that exists because nobody divulges every aspect of his or her life to another.

Acceptable excuses for infidelity are not excuses, which can be used over and over. They are excuses, which can lead their partners to forgiving them or having their partners, if nothing else, understand. Relationships between family members and a married couple are for lack of a better word, bad and by this I mean a man messing around with his sister in law or vise versa. There are almost no acceptable or forgivable excuses for sleeping with a married member of one's family, except for the identical twins and triplets situation. While these types of people may share every physical attribute, they may not share the same amount of morals. A person who has one or two twin brothers could have just gotten married to the girl of his dreams. That girl of one brother's dreams could be a nightmare to the other brother. One brother could pretend to be the married brother in order to have sex with the wife. People are evil like that. Now I know many of you are probably saying 'well if the wife is married to the twin or has been married to the twin brother for a significant amount of time, then she should be able to instantly recognize the difference between the two. Now that does make quite a bit of sense but what about the situation of alcohol? What if the wife is one that frequently indulges and at the time of this particular indiscretion, she was very much under the influence and her judgment as they say was impaired? The other brother may quickly find out or may never find out at all. He could kill his brother or hate him for eternity but he would not rightfully be able to hold anger toward the significant other. People do many evil things in this world and people make honest and sometimes stupid mistakes. A person must always explore the reasons why certain actions were committed before passing judgment or punishment.

Chapter Eight
Effects Of Infidelity

Infidelity or being 'natural' as I like to call it has many causes. Lack of morals, unhappiness and sexual incompatibility are just a small portion of the massive number of reasons some people may feel the need to cheat. There are several remedies, which can help like therapy, revenge sex or even separation but some of the effects of infidelity sometimes outlast the proposed cure. The effects of infidelity are many and can include hatred of the entire gender, as with separation. The effects can also include mixed or confused feelings, as what could come from certain types of therapy. I like to call therapy confusing because even though by definition, therapy is the treatment of physical, mental or behavioral problems, there is always the possibility that the person conducting the therapy may miss the mark. They may be able to decipher some of the issues, which cause many people to cheat, however those issues could be totally contradictory to the issues in your specific situation. The effects could also send a person to jail because infidelity and its associations, such as bigamy, are illegal in certain provinces. Infidelity can even cause an unwanted life to be brought into the world as what could happen with revenge sex. As I often like to mention, fate has a sometimes totally twisted sense of humor. Fate will allow infidelity to enter into a couple's relationship. It will allow the couple to eventually get past the indiscretion but may cause the innocent party in the relationship to desire revenge. The innocent party who has a vengeance driven affair, with the help of fate, will either become pregnant or end up getting somebody outside the relationship pregnant and we all know what happens then, a family is created, a family is destroyed, somebody gets killed or there is an appearance on a nationwide talk show. The effects of infidelity are often quite varied. They can range from desirable to undesirable and from temporary to lifelong. Under desirable, one of the effects as stated by some individuals who have committed infidelity and lived to tell about it would have to be the unmatched feeling of 'new.' Sleeping with somebody totally different - different body structure, different voice, even different movements in the bedroom are all a part of 'new.' The fact that this new person maybe morally, religiously and possibly, legally unavailable just adds to the feeling of excitement. Another desirable effect of infidelity is the 'immediate celebrity status' which people who commit infidelity are likely to receive. Let's say this couple, Ryan & Tasha are married and let's also say that there is a woman named Kim, whom every man in the neighborhood has a physical attraction to. Unfortunately, none of these men are able to capture her interest. If Ryan steps outside the bounds of fidelity and has a successful affair with Kim, he will instantly be viewed as an icon. He will be thought of as the person that has his cake and is able to eat it too. This 'status' is highly desired because in relationships, many times people are 'forgotten.' They are viewed as unhappy drones with no capacity for logical or individual thought. In short, they are thought of as unhappy because they are in a relationship. When these people are able to promulgate an affair, for a certain period of time and without the knowledge of their partner, they become what everybody in an unhappy or stagnant relationship wishes they could, envied. Desirable effects can also describe the short-lived escape from the problems of an unhappy relationship. Every relationship has or will have its fair share of problems. People will use certain remedies to escape from those problems. Most often those remedies come in the form of stress relievers – and many of those stress relievers come in the form of drug & alcohol abuse or another person. Drugs and alcohol have an extremely colorful reputation when it comes to relieving stress and eradicating unpleasant memories. Indulging in an affair with someone outside of the unhappy relationship has also long provided the necessary outlet for frustration as well as mental anguish. The unfortunate side about the desirable effects of infidelity is that as good as they may make someone feel, the effects are almost always temporary. The problems, just like when a person indulges in drugs, alcohol or cheating, will still remain after the good feeling is gone. On some rare occasions, the good feeling, which is provided by the three previous examples, can actually add to the problems the drugs, alcohol & cheating were attempting to eradicate. Smoking marijuana and/or drinking, for example causes a person to have lapses in memory - among other medical issues. 'Forgetting' has always been used as a potential tactic for escaping the consequences of an infidelity interrogation. This tactic, like everything else in life has its advantages and disadvantages. Here's an example; what if hypothetical couple Ryan & Tasha were the type of people to argue at least three times a week and instead of going to therapy or attempting to work out their problems in a civilized manner, Ryan smokes a few joints every time they fight and Tasha gets on the phone with her girlfriends. Ryan's ability to remember that he was supposed to pick up his son from school at twelve o'clock instead of at three o'clock could be severely hampered by his indulgence; thereby leading to another argument on top of whatever he and Tasha were arguing about before. Tasha's girlfriends will more than likely, have no problem in assisting her belief that Ryan 'forgot' on purpose – even going so far as to lead Tasha into believing that Ryan's tardiness was due to him screwing around with some other woman. Having relations with someone new is always desirable, however it is very possible for some of those new people to have serious, deep-rooted issues. While you may be thinking this new person can provide the elusive 'relief' you so desperately need to help make your relationship bearable, this new person may be thinking you are their soul mate. Heaven forbid you and this person have sex and they become 'whipped' to the point of 'psychotic – ness.' If this happens, you may never be able to rid yourself or your relationship of them.

Some of the undesirable effects of infidelity, as told to me by some of those who have gotten caught are new found hatred, broken trust and loss of benefits. The newfound hatred, coupled with feelings of betrayal will drive the relationship from the point of cheating, onward. Many will agree that a person's heart is the most sensitive part of their body. When broken it takes longer to heal than all others. If a person were to break an arm, resetting the bone, adding a cast and resting a few weeks should be all that is necessary to get things back to normal. If a person were to break a leg, pretty much the same treatment. The heart however, if broken, can remain that way for an actual lifetime. The main reason this effect is so undesirable is that if a person's broken heart is never properly treated, that person will carry along hatred through every consecutive relationship they find themselves involved in. Infidelity has the capability to eradicate all traces of relationship trust. Trust is not just one of the components of a happy and successful relationship; trust is an essential part of any happy and successful relationship. Once the bond of trust is broken, you have nothing. A person can be part of a relationship which has been challenged by an affair and say they forgive their partner but how will they respond when the memory or something which triggers a memory, challenges that forgiveness?

One of the most noticeable effects of infidelity is losing a relationship all together. Many people have no tolerance whatsoever for cheating. These people will cut off any connection to the person who cheated as well as attempt to cut off any available part of that person's anatomy. This can be seen as a definite loss of benefits because if there are children involved, the innocent party may not want to allow the guilty party the privilege of seeing or visiting them. Then we all know what happens – six months to a year or more of family court just to get that evil bitch or cruel motherfucker to let you see your kids. Then there's the visit by the probation department to make sure you have a suitable home for your kids. Then you have some ignorant fucking law guardian interviewing the kids to see if they want to see you. The bad part about this is that kids may think its fun to say no. I know there are some people reading this who may reason that if parents are going through unhappiness, the kids would desire to be with both but what if the parents were the type to disagree amicably? What if the kids never knew anything was actually wrong or what if the kids knew something was wrong but were not aware of to what extent? What if for some reason or other the kids just happen to be mad at dad? Kids may also just be having a bad day or bad week or bad month. The really bad part about this is that the ignorant people doing the investigation will not always take the necessary time needed to decipher the child's true feelings. What many people don't know, especially those who do not have children, is that they need to be guided, not just raised but directed in the proper way to go. If you give a young child an ultimatum, chances are they will not weigh the positives against the negatives, they will not say this is better for me in the long run, chances are they will say ' enie, meenie, minie mo' and choose whatever sounds or seems nice at the time. A three, four or five year old can play an adult just as well as an adult can play another but people don't always want to read into situations they way they should be read. They want to accept whatever is told to them – and why shouldn't they, it's not their child. These individuals, in their infinite wisdom, will report to some over worked, non caring judge, that the child shows little interest or desire to see the parent, which will cause the jackass of a judge to say okay, you can only see your child one hour a fucking week – or some dumb shit like that. The good part is that eventually you will get to see them. The bad part about this is that by the time you do get to finally see your children, it will be too late for you to have an effective part in their upbringing and chances are your kids will grow up more like the significant other you hate instead of having qualities the both of you exude and could be proud of. All this, just because you could not keep your clothes on. Sometimes you have to ask yourself, is a roll in the hay really worth all the potential drama? If you are hell bent on being natural and you have weighed the options and feel you have more to gain than lose, then by all means have a ball – but remember something, cheating is just like losing your virginity. Once you do it, you cannot get back your innocence or your self-respect. If you're okay with that, like I said before – have a ball.

If you are dependent upon your partner for whatever reason, like say for car payments or for help with your child's school tuition, infidelity, rather getting caught in the act of infidelity will more often than not make the person you were dependent on have a change of heart in regards to continuing the financial assistance. Infidelity can cause depression. It can cause a person to question his or her self worth. The effects of infidelity can stretch from physical to emotional and beyond. One of the most undesirable effects of infidelity is infidelity's uncanny ability to make a person jaded. When a person becomes jaded in regards to the opposite sex, they may no longer find interest in them or in relationships altogether. This jaded feeling can confuse others into thinking that a person is anti social, gay or lesbian. This jaded feeling can make a man feel all women are bitches. It can make a woman feel that all men ain't shit. Being jaded can change a person's way of thinking permanently. Infidelity has more power than people give it credit for. Many of the people who are unwilling participants in affairs (the innocent parties) very rarely are left with the feeling that maybe my partner just had a weak moment or maybe they just wanted to experiment. <u>Infidelity will make even the most level headed, open minded person believe that the guilty party either had intentions on cheating all along or was never in love with the significant other to begin with.</u> Infidelity will make the innocent party believe that the guilty party has no redeeming qualities other than the ability to wiggle his pee pee or spread her legs to whomever requests or allows them. As with most things in life, the few make it bad for the many. Sexually transmitted diseases are an undesirable by product of infidelity people do not like to discuss. As if the act of cheating by itself is not bad enough, there is always the possibility of the transmission of syphilis, gonorrhea or worse. Some people in relationships who cheat on their partners and find out that they have a sexually transmitted disease often try and hide that fact from their partner. This is attempted because nine times out of ten, if one partner was to inform the other that they have a sexually transmitted disease, that partner would try and kill him or her. This is a very popular by product of infidelity people often overlook when indulging in affairs. Many people who cheat are often caught up in the moment - they get the feeling, then act on it. Many of these people who live in the moment have no idea of the sexual history of the person they sleep with. This is nothing new, most of the people who have sex nowadays rarely, if ever inquire about their partners' sexual history but the problem is that these people are already in relationships and are putting their partners' lives and potential happiness in jeopardy. There are a few who take precautions, wearing condoms & such but there are many more who don't and these are the ones who need to be castrated or killed. Here's a worst-case scenario: a couple is married and one of them decides to have an affair. That person who initiates the affair may contract a sexually transmitted disease from the extra marital relationship. That man or woman brings back the disease to the husband or wife. If they have a child, that child will more than likely be born with that sexually transmitted disease as well. If the person outside the relationship who brought the disease into the lives of the committed couple was to have a child with someone else, then that's a total of at least six people contracting an STD from one. The effects of infidelity are quite harsh ain't they?

Chapter Nine
Situations Which Resemble Infidelity

All too often people in relationships are 'on guard' when it comes to the actions of their partners. They trust but they don't trust. Some of them are looking and hoping to find that one thing, which will push the relationship over the edge, causing them to breakup. That one thing, more often than not is infidelity. People who are 'on guard' about their partner's activities will search wallets, purses, coat pockets, even going so far as to check phone records – all so that they can confirm their suspicions, break up with their cheating partners and forever be able to say 'I'm not the one who got caught!' Causes of this raised defense level can range from prior bouts of infidelity to being raised with the belief that the opposite sex is unworthy or incapable of trust. Insecurity is also a very possible but often overlooked factor. In a relationship, a person is not just dealing with another person. Many times, they are dealing with that person's family, that person's own beliefs and the beliefs instilled in that person from his or her family. If there are negative beliefs in a relationship, such as 'men are dogs and they always eventually cheat' a person may find himself consistently fighting that belief as well as consistently trying to provide a happy and positive environment. If a man is involved in a relationship with a woman who believes as above, that man, if he wants a happy union will have to do, not what will be considered the right thing for him but do what the woman believes is the right and necessary thing to alleviate suspicion for her. Sometimes women have astronomical requirements for a man to comply with in order to prove or maintain his innocence – even if he has done nothing wrong. This can include having the man come straight home after work – every single, godforsaken day. This can also include the man not being able to associate with another female unless it is in the presence of his significant other. This is an unfortunate level of control, which the deviation from can resemble infidelity and is often what causes a relationship to go sour. Common sense dictates that people should not involve themselves in a relationship, where there are potential signs for future craziness or immediate relationship failure. What common sense does not dictate is how a person's level of attractiveness will almost always override common sense. Very few people have relationships without parental or 'best friend' interference. Parental and best friend <u>assistance</u> regarding relationships can often be a good thing. However, when that assistance becomes interference, it then becomes time to distance one's self from that type of meddling. The problem many people in relationships have is that they do not always know when one changes into the other.

Being aware of potential indiscretions is always a good thing but when a person lets that awareness rule their lives and future relationships, its no longer reasonable concern, its paranoia. One thing, which can fuel this type of paranoia, is the inability to distinguish actual infidelity from the situations, which resemble infidelity. Some of those situations are

1) A change in sex patterns
2) Spending more time with the opposite sex
3) Baby mama & baby daddy syndrome
4) Guilt by association
5) Late night & hang up calls
6) Forgetfulness
7) Calling someone else's name

A change in sex patterns - People in relationships, for the most part, have a certain schedule or special time when it comes to intimacy. This special time could be after the kids go to bed or on the weekends or Monday, Wednesday and Friday. This special time comes into play because the longer a relationship stretches; the less the chance for spontaneity exists. When a relationship is new, certain people have sex all the time but as time goes on, quite often, the physical intimacy must be scheduled around children and family, careers and friends. When there is doubt about the fidelity of someone in a relationship, a partner's suspicions can be fueled by any action the other may make. If for instance, a couple has been together for a few months or even a few years and they have a regularly scheduled intimacy routine of every Monday, Wednesday &

Friday after the kids go to bed, it would be highly suspect if all of a sudden, one partner only desires intimacy on Friday. The reasons for the lapse could be anything from overexertion from work to being sick of the monotonous love making schedule but if there is already suspicion, infidelity will be the first thing to enter the other's mind. The change in sex patterns will resemble infidelity because people generally view sex as one of the most, if not the most important part of a relationship. If, without explanation, a change is instituted, the other partner is very likely to think that outside influence of the male or female variety is taking up the slack.

When it comes to the sexual part of relationships, there is often very little preparation. People expect their partners and significant others to always be ready. Rarely do people take into account factors, such as age, health, work schedule or interest. Many people think 'hey, if I feel like doing it, you should too!' or 'if you don't feel like doing it, you should make yourself ready to do it just to appease me.' This belief, combined with the factors stated above, are the main reasons many infidelity-resembling situations, exist. The sexual prowess of many men, for instance deteriorates greatly with age. This can cause these men to use Viagra the same way an average six year old child would use candy. This can also cause daily sexual exploits to become monthly sexual exploits. A woman, who does not understand that prostate problems may lead to sexual dysfunction, may more than likely believe that a particular man is cheating because of his change in the amount of physical intimacy. Work schedules, as well as the type of employment a person has, can confuse a person about actual infidelity and a situation, which resembles it. A person may work sixty hours a week, instead of the widely accepted forty, like most other people. This extra twenty hours is basically the same thing as working a week and a half in the time allotted for one week of work. Most people will desire nothing more than sleep, peace and quiet after an extended labor load such as this. A person involved with someone who works this much may believe the other's inability to engage in physical intimacy as often as the other would like is due to them possibly having an affair at the workplace or an affair in general. There is also the possibility that a person only works a regular forty-hour week but has such a stress filled position that they are too frazzled to enjoy a peaceful and intimate evening at home as often as the other would like. This may cause the other to think that they are losing interest or are just being natural. People in relationships rarely want to give the benefit of the doubt to the person they are involved with – especially when it comes to the possibility of infidelity. One of the most popular reasons this exists is because people expect their partners to be perfect. They expect them to not be capable of doing wrong. When the reality sets in that the person these people are dealing with is not superhuman, every belief in the world which will lead the other to think that infidelity is actually occurring will be bestowed on the tired or stressed out partner.

<u>Spending more time with the opposite sex</u> – Affairs, for the most part are initiated or perpetrated by a member of the opposite sex of one of the parties in a relationship. If a man and woman are committed and infidelity rears its ugly head, chances are that it will be either another man sneaking around with the woman or another woman sneaking around with the man. As of late, there is this thing about 'down low' people who have sex with their significant others and have relations with members of the same sex also. This is mainly a male problem, hence the term 'down low brother' but women have these types of relations too. Only difference, it doesn't seem to be as widespread or as big a deal. For the purpose of this book, I'll stick with infidelity as meaning the traditional way – sleeping with someone of the opposite sex, while you're in a commitment. The biggest fear of married and committed people is friends. This is usually because friends are the ones who spend the most amount of time with a person besides the significant other. Friends know when you are going through good times as well as bad. Friends often have a pretty good idea of your finances as well as a good portion of your inner most secrets. The point I am trying to make is that as wonderful as friends can actually be, they are equally dangerous. In most committed relationships, there are usually other committed couples that fit the bill as far as friends. For instance, Ryan and Tasha may be married, as are Kim and David. Being that Ryan and David are both males, they become the best of friends. Kim and Tasha do the same. There is no problem until Ryan and Tasha have relationship difficulties and begin spending time with their opposite sex best friends. Ryan and Kim start spending time together alone, talking mainly about the unhappiness in Ryan and Tasha's relationship and David and Tasha start to wonder why. The wonder can lead to suspicion. The suspicion can lead to accusation. The accusation can lead to arguments, which can lead to Ryan and Kim being closer than friends should be. David and Tasha will see this and suspect that Ryan and Kim are doing more than what they actually are, which may in fact just be talking. This can lead David and Tasha to being more than just friends. This situation can also happen with one couple and a single person. The most common instance I have seen is the stay at home wife who finally gets a job and becomes friends with the boss or the office flirt. When a married woman starts to associate herself with a single man, even if the relationship is 100% platonic, there will be feelings of concern. The same will hold true for a married man associating himself with a single woman. The power of trust will have very little power in this equation but a person must be steadfast. There can be as close to complete trust as possible but the fact still remains, when infidelity or the possibility of is dangled in front of someone's face, that someone will sit up and take notice. The big belief among many people is that if a married person has a close, single friend, that single friend will always, ever so subtly, be trying to move in on the married person's territory. The single friend will always 'be there' for the married friend in times of need and especially when the married friend's significant other 'acts up.' This belief exists mainly because throughout history, scumbags (and I can think of no better word to describe them) have always been hanging around a person in a relationship just in case there was an argument which lasted a little too long or a period of unhappiness which seemed too apparent or a separation which caused a person to divulge his or her desire for companionship. It's the same philosophy behind these ambulance chaser lawyers who look for accidents (mostly by following ambulances) and upon reaching an accident scene, hand out business cards saying 'I'm a lawyer, call me.' They solicit business the same way the scumbags above solicit sex. It should be stated that not all single people who have married friends are looking to jump into their pants. As I tell folks all the time there are many good people in this world who are labeled bad because of association or because of historical beliefs. In a relationship as in life, one of the most difficult questions to answer is why. A person can watch another and figure out what and how. That person can also figure out where and when. It will take an exceptionally intuitive individual however to figure out why. People like the ones described above can call the home of a married person every single day but if there is no understanding of why, then suspicion will definitely set in. This situation may be the furthest thing from infidelity but as long as it is not dispelled and dispelled in a timely manner, then it will be thought of as such.

There is also a situation, which deals with time spent away from the significant other altogether. Many people feel that no matter what the issue, a couple never needs time apart. These people feel that a person's love is contingent upon how much time said person spends with a significant other. This is ludicrous. This is nonsense. This is straight up bullshit. Anybody in a relationship will or at least should be able to tell you that the longer a couple is together, the more time away from one another they will desire and need. In The Correct Way To Fool Around part one, I mentioned that for success or at least happiness, everything should be done in moderation and I believe this is nowhere truer than in relationships. It is a well known fact that if a couple is around one another every single, godforsaken day, then eventually, sometimes sooner than later, they will tire of each other. On the same note, if a couple does not spend enough time together, one, if not both will desire some form of companionship from someone else. Ladies, wanna find out if a man is lying? Ask him if he ever wants to spend time away from you. Ask him if he wouldn't rather have a couple of hours each week just to himself or just to hang out with friends he grew up with and hasn't seen in years. Ask him if you get on his fucking nerves. If he says no, then you have yourself a definite liar. This situation resembles infidelity because many people feel that any time spent away from a significant other is prime opportunity for cheating. This is pretty much a no win situation. Freedom or independence in a relationship is something everybody <u>needs</u> to have but it something that many feeble and insecure minds will chastise the person they are involved with for <u>attempting</u> to have. People in these relationships, who have small and feeble minds, will call the significant other excessively. If they live apart, they will stop by the significant others home unannounced. They will do a boatload of things just to ensure that this situation, which resembles infidelity, is nothing more than a resemblance of infidelity. They will give their significant others time away from them in the physical presence sense but will keep in contact with them through every other medium possible to make sure he or she is not fooling around.

One of the more recognizable situations, which resemble infidelity, is **the baby mama and baby daddy syndrome.** This is a situation where a person has a child and that person is no longer involved with that child's mother or father and there are problems, which come about because of that fact. As with all other situations dealing with or resembling infidelity, a great deal of trust is necessary to move past the unsure period. People who have children and then separate themselves from that child's birth parent are only separating themselves by distance. From the time that child is born, the mother and father will be connected to him or her and each other, whether or not the step parent likes it. The fact that most parents will take care of their children at any and all costs can resemble infidelity because taking care of a child will usually subject both of the child's parents to be in close, if not constant contact with one another. This is where insecurities cause relationships to break up or at least have problems. People know that having a child is a life-changing event. What these people don't always realize is that that life-changing event applies to both of the parents. Again, there has to be trust because you as a separated parent can hate the very air your significant other breathes – and your new husband or wife can fully know this. If however, your child, whom you love dearly requests your presence at a family event or other special occasion, at which the child's custodial parent happens to be, if there is not a sufficient level of trust, accusations from the new significant other, to the effect of 'you're probably still sleeping with him or her' may present themselves. There is always the possibility and in some circles, the belief that once a child is conceived, the parents of that child will always have a sexual relationship with one another – and that sexual or parental attraction will always supercede any future relationship the two of them will ever have. In layman's terms, 'I'm the baby's daddy, so any relationship you have, as well as any relationship you will ever have will be insignificant to what we had.' This belief, in essence can be a springboard for sex. This, for the perpetually dumb, is not a situation, which resembles infidelity. This is infidelity. It must be stated that a person's original parents will always have some level of importance. Whether that level takes precedence over future relationships is strictly up to the custodial parent. There are people who like to sugarcoat things to the effect of 'even though another man is my child's father, I consider you his dad' just because the other man takes care of him but the fact still remains - good acts do not make a parent, unprotected sex does. This does not mean that just because a couple has children together, they will always be having sex, even after they break up - that is just a belief held by many. A person who has a child with another will always have, if not a relationship, then a lifelong connection with that person, through the child.

Another situation, which often resembles infidelity, is what's commonly called **guilt by association**. It is a well-known fact that most of the people who initiate infidelity are often the outgoing, fun types, who are always searching for the next big thrill. It's also a well known fact that these people almost always have a friend on the opposite side of the spectrum, meaning dull or if not dull, then not as exciting as they themselves are. The same holds true for attractive people having a not so attractive friend. Attractive people sometimes have not as attractive friends for their other desirable attributes, such as intelligence or dependability. The reason each group has their selected choice of friends can vary, from the attractive people choosing less pretty friends so that their appearance based and shallow boyfriends or girlfriends won't be attracted to them, to the exciting ones picking boring friends for the belief that the boring ones will never leave their side for fear of losing the only exciting person or people in their lives. The exciting and attractive people do share one thing in common; they are usually the ones involved in affairs more often than their not so attractive and not as exciting counterparts. This can, to an extent be a good thing, because if a person is involved with someone unattractive or boring, chances will not be that great that they will be involved in that many affairs. However, there is always the other hand and on the other hand people who seem unattractive to one person will almost definitely seem attractive to someone else. The same thing is true for people who are classified as boring. There is this saying; one person's trash is another's treasure. That simply means what one person does not want, the next person or the next few people may. The fact that unattractive and boring people are less likely to be involved in a majority of affairs can, to an extent be a bad thing as well. Because the friend of someone is always doing something wrong, people will almost automatically assume that whomever associates with him or her is doing wrong as well. Assumptions have destroyed many a relationship and will continue to do so because as long as assumptions are unchallenged, people will believe them and allow them to lead their interpretations of others. Here's a for instance; if a person has a friend who is very popular in the entertainment industry, people will assume that the celebrity has money and assume that the friend has money as well – even if the friend is not known to have so much as a job. If a man is seen with a multitude of different woman, on many occasions, the assumption will be that that man is promiscuous, even if he is a virgin. If a woman has a friend who everybody refers to as the town whore, people will assume that that woman's quiet friend will have certain shared characteristics, even if not publicly known. Assumptions fuel guilt by association cases and once a person has a certain belief in his or her mind; the hardest thing in the world is garnering the effort necessary to remove that belief.

Sooner or later we all have to fit ourselves into society's accepted activities for specific age groups or gender. Those who do not conform risk being ostracized or classified as individuals outside the realm of normalcy. A better word would be weird. This in itself can be a situation, which resembles infidelity. For instance, a man wearing a historically feminine color, such as lavender or pink, would by some people, automatically be thought of as gay. A senior citizen, riding or attempting to ride a scooter built for a child, would be interpreted by most as someone with serious psychological problems. A young child, who would rather stay home on a hot summer day and study as opposed to going outdoors to play or to a pool, would be thought of as either having certain phobias, problems or very strict discipline. As stated before, people make judgments and assumptions based on what they see and on what they believe to be 'normal' for a specific age group and/or gender. These beliefs do not have to be necessarily true because some people make a habit of going against the norm. Some men may wear pink or lavender shirts and be as straight as an arrow. They may do so because they are either trying to make a bold fashion statement or because they just don't give a damn about anybody else's opinion. (Then again there could be the case of them actually not knowing that those colors are historically reserved for women, gay people and men who can fight very well.) An old man riding a scooter built for a child may raise many eyebrows when it comes to his senility or state of mind - but what's rarely thought of is that maybe the old man just feels like acting like a child. Some people have the type of minds, which can rival some of our greatest philosophers, yet human nature often causes us to desire to retain the playfulness of our youth. People are many times under the illusion that how someone portrays himself or herself is the only way that person is ever allowed to act. The same holds true for a child who would rather stay home on a hot summer day. That action does not automatically mean the child is weird or under some strict, Adolph Hitler type of rule, that child may just enjoy doing schoolwork. (Then again, maybe he is weird!) A person's actions do not always dictate who they are. Sometimes those actions dictate who they want you to believe them to be. When people do what's not usually expected of them, they often attract attention. Attention for example, is one of the biggest enemies to criminals, whether those criminals are breaking a law or breaking a heart. Some people do things just to attract attention, like the ever popular, attempting to make a significant other jealous. This situation resembles infidelity more than any other because the guise of infidelity is often used to make a significant other believe infidelity is present. The reason a person may use this tactic can vary from wanting that person to pay more attention in the relationship to getting back at that person for flirting a bit too much. How well this tactic works is disputable because often the possibility exists that a person who is made jealous will cheat just because he or she thinks that the other party who has made him or her jealousies actually cheating.

Late night and hang up calls – The telephone is undoubtedly the greatest communication device ever! Talk to somebody across the street, across the country or across the world, just by pressing a few buttons, how simply wonderful is that? Unfortunately as with every good thing in this world, there is an equal and opposite bad. The bad thing about the telephone is not an issue related to its operation but issues relating to the use and abuse of its operation. People in relationships have what's called unwritten rules for the longevity and success of togetherness. These rules vary in length from couple to couple but they are put in place to basically 'keep each other in check.' These rules are the equivalent of lines, which if crossed, will activate hidden jealousy, start an argument or just make the other person say hmmm. (Hmmm is the equivalent of suspicion) One of the most basic rules couples need to and should adhere to once they become involved is the eradication of **the late night phone call.** Phone calls after a certain hour have been historically linked to sexual activity or activities leading to sexual activity. A two a.m. phone call to a woman who is in a relationship by a man, who is not a relative, is either an emergency or a booty call. That is the popular belief and that belief is very justified. What other possible excuse or reason can there be? When a couple becomes involved, there are changes. Sometimes there are life changes but most times there are lifestyle changes. Lifestyle changes include consulting with another before making decisions, which affect your life. They also include putting someone else's feelings first. This means thinking about how whatever action you are doing or are about to undertake will make your partner feel. People must act like they are in a relationship because if people in a relationship act as if they are single, then few will respect their relationship. In regards to relationships, unless there is a shared business, (which happens to be open 24hours) there is no logical or feasible reason for someone to call at that time of night. Casual conversation has a cutoff time and once that time has passed, any call received by a friend of either party will be viewed as crossing the line. This situation resembles infidelity because as stated previously, what reasonable explanations can a person have except for emergencies when calling at two in the morning? Everybody has friends. Sometimes these friends are friends of both parties in a relationship and sometimes these friends are just friends of one. One thing friends like to do is hang out on occasion. This hanging out can be going to a movie, dinner or even just a walk with nowhere particular in mind. Now in most relationships, where there is a decent level of trust, not even an eyebrow of suspicion should be raised if one party in a relationship says to the other 'hon, I'm going to the movies with so & so tomorrow night – even if so & so is a member of the opposite sex. As long as both parties are okay with it, it should not be a problem. This does not mean that a husband's wife should always be hanging out with somebody else, even if the husband knows and is good friends with this person. It just means that if the husband can't attend the event with his wife and the person whom they both know and trust is willing and able, there should be not that much of a problem. The problem comes in when so & so decides to call at three a.m. and ask a person in a relationship (who just happens to live with his or her significant other) if he or she wants to go clubbing. Unless both parties are heavily into the club scene and are people who regularly make a habit of going out with each other's friends at all hours of the day and night (which I personally think is crazy) this call will be interpreted as if not an action which may possibly lead to cheating, then disrespect in its most basic form.

Hang up calls are just as problematic. The thing about hang up calls is just like secrets, if a person does not know the full story or the reason behind them, usually that person will allow his or her mind to wander. Hang up calls always seem to have the uncanny ability of seeking out couples that are experiencing turmoil in their relationship. This particular couple could be battling the thought of infidelity. There could be no proof to the accusations and the arguments could be purely circumstantial based but something as small as a person calling from a blocked number and not saying anything could drive those assumptions wild. People in their infinite wisdom <u>want</u> to believe certain things. Some people want to believe that most of the people in this world are generally good. Others want to believe that most men are dogs and some people are inclined to believe that members of particular races all share the same attributes – whether those attributes are good or bad. When people have these certain beliefs in their minds, usually they desire nothing more than confirmation, whether that confirmation is correct or not. That confirmation can come in the form of a nosey best friend, a talk show audience or a not completely reliable lie detector test. People who are in a 'disbelieving' zone will have no room for reasonable and logical thought. They will believe what they want to believe and nothing else. There is something, which kids have been doing since I was a kid and probably many years before – it is the practice of calling someone whom they do not know and attempting to have that person stay on the phone as long as possible. Kids will do this because they're either bored or mischievous or both. The goal of this phone marathon competition is supposed to be that whoever keeps a person talking the longest is the winner. What the result often ends up being however is a disrupted or ended relationship. Some people will feel that the calls are being made by someone their significant other knows and this needn't be the case. Some people who play this game will call a person back many times depending upon that person's initial response. Let's say for instance, if you were to get a call from someone who had no purpose other than to keep you on the phone talking nonsense and you, not particularly in the mood for nonsense, offer this person the opportunity to have sex with themselves, that person may call you back again and again until they get tired. All a jealous spouse or lover would have to do is answer the phone when the person you pissed off feels like calling repeatedly and hanging up. Whether or not you explain that you have no idea who this person is, if your lover witnesses you on the phone, he or she may likely believe that you actually know this bored, lonely or psychotic individual. This situation resembles infidelity because the thought of infidelity not only exists but also thrives on mistaken and unproven beliefs. If you are the type of person who believes one thing and is unwilling to listen to listen to any other explanation or possibility, then someone like the kids above can mess up or end your relationship. It cannot be stated enough; <u>trust</u> will counteract any situation, which resembles infidelity. Unfortunately many people feel that relationships are mainly liaisons of convenience. These people are not so willing to trust but are willing to become involved in relationships. Ironic isn't it? Especially when <u>trust is one of the basic foundations for any decent relationship.</u> The fact that many people in this world cannot be or refuse to be alone will make them prematurely involve themselves in relationships, which they are not emotionally or sometimes mentally ready for.

<u>Forgetfulness</u> – the process of actual or implied mental deterioration. Forgetfulness resembles infidelity because it is usually the first and most often used excuse when someone in a relationship, who has doubt about the integrity of their partner, questions them. Forgetfulness is more than 'I forget what happened that night.' Forgetfulness is specific, as in saying 'I went to see John last month on the 16th, then we hung out at the 40/40 club till about 1am, then I took a taxi to my cousin's house and slept off all of the alcohol – when in actuality the person in question went to John's house on the 17th, hung out at the Roxy, then got a ride from one of the people he or she met at the club. Certain things are factors in forgetfulness; for instance age.

The older a person gets, the less they remember. There are also some diseases and ailments, which can hinder a person's ability to remember, such as Alzheimer's disease or HIV. In the case above, alcohol or the over indulgence of can make someone unwittingly distort facts they think are accurate. Someone who does not drink or who has a picture perfect type memory may think that the other person, instead of actually forgetting, is lying. The wonderful thing about forgetfulness is that it can be exploited. People can use it because it is one of the reasons given for infidelity and that it is almost impossible to prove. If a person is lying when questioned about infidelity and they mix facts up intentionally, it may temporarily help them escape a bad situation because almost everybody, at one time or another has forgotten something. The questioning party may accept this excuse because they may feel everybody is human and entitled to forget something once in a while. The bad part about using the forgetfulness excuse is that 1, you will have to remember when you used it as well as the fact that you used it as opposed to telling the truth or some other excuse and 2, if you use the forgetfulness excuse a lot you will have to remember to ration it out among daily activities otherwise you risk having people think you actually do have a condition which needs looking into. People are very perceptive when it comes to certain things. If you only use the forgetfulness excuse when you are in trouble, chances are very good that your partner will pick up on that. If you play forgetful enough and on a regular basis, your partner will start to believe that you might be possibly be suffering from brain failure. A good thing? Maybe but the down side to this is that you will have to remember each lie you told in an attempt to make your partner believe you couldn't remember.

Calling someone else's name can be a result of forgetfulness. It can also be a result of association or basic confusion. People who have two or more children often name them with names, which begin with the same letter. Some people do this because they believe it is easier for others to remember their names and some people do it just because it sounds cute. This can be confusing because if the names are closely related such as Tom & Tim, a stressful situation can cause a person to easily mix up the two. If two kids or grown people for that matter have similar traits or identical features, they can be confused because they look or act alike. This is one of the most common instances of situations, which resemble infidelity because people think that anytime someone makes this type of mistake, they are thinking about the other person in either a sexual or not completely platonic manner. I have two friends – one named Lisa and one named Leslie and I always find myself confusing the two. They do get upset and I am ever so thankful that I am not in a relationship with either of them because trying to explain to somebody that calling them another's name is just a simple mistake is one of the hardest things in the world.

Often people go to strip clubs. The reasons vary in intensity but the bottom line is something is missing. It could be that the relationship just needs a little rejuvenation or the individual who frequents these types of establishments has a fetish for seeing the opposite sex naked. If a person in a relationship goes to a strip club and is 'rejuvenated' to the point where the memory of that dancer stays on the other's mind, it's possible that that person may blurt out that stripper's name during moments of intimacy with that person's significant other. People get mad when they feel their partner is not fully focused on them at all times but to be completely honest, how many people **always** only think of their significant others when they are having sex with them? Not as many as most would think. It is quite possible that a person who has just left or recently left a strip club is on his or her way home to make mad passionate love to their significant other, all while thinking of the person at the club. Yes it is almost the same as sleeping with the stripper but most would agree that thinking about doing something is much less damaging than the actual act. This is especially true when one person has wronged another and the person who was wronged desires nothing more than to beat the living shit out of the person who has wronged him or her. I'll be the first to tell you that it feels good – so good sometimes to think about doing what was stated above but thinking about it and doing it are two different things. Sometimes when a person leaves a strip club he or she is so hot and bothered that the sex with the significant other is better than it normally is when there is no stripper intervention. I see this as a win-win. Think about it; husband goes out to get a little stimulation. Wife wants attention when husband comes home. The husband comes home and bangs the wife into next week all while thinking of the porn star look a like he saw or had a lap dance with at the club. Now here's the bad part: The husband, in a moment of overwhelming ecstasy calls out candy instead of Kathy. The wife will be very happy that she is getting good sex but she will more than likely be pissed about the mistaken moniker. This can lead the wife to believe that instead of the husband just going to the strip club to see some naked women then come home with an erection, the husband had sex with at least one girl named candy. This allegation does not have to be proven. The fact that the husband was in fact thinking about a woman named candy, in whatever capacity, is enough to fuel the suspicions of the wife. Many people try to control a person's mind then get feverishly upset when they can't. This is one of the things, which leads to infidelity. For instance; some hypocrites I know do not want their significant others to frequent strip clubs or any place where a stripper or scantily clad individual will be. Yet these people will go to any and every strip club, bar or sex party they can find. These hypocrites do not realize that whenever there is a longing for something and that longing is suppressed, it will only resurface and quite possibly with a stronger desire than before. These are the people who don't know how to act when they get around strippers – even going so far as to actually pay to have sex with them. Now I am not saying that if you let a person go to a strip club whenever he or she desires that it will cut down on infidelity, I am saying that whenever a person is not allowed to make himself or herself happy because of restrictions set forth by the other person in the relationship, that person will be more inclined to try to make happiness the ultimate goal at the first given opportunity. A person's body can be controlled as easily as a puppet but a person's mind is his or her own. That person can think about everything from screwing one to screwing five hundred but as long as no action is perpetrated, the situation will forever be nothing more than one, which resembles infidelity.

Another situation, which resembles infidelity is dumbness – or if not dumbness, then naiveté to the point of retardation. People who seem less intelligent than most or who are completely believing in the good of man are often tricked into certain situations. One of those situations is the 'he wants to have sex with you' 'no he doesn't, he's just being nice' thing. Many in relationships often have conversations of this nature. Reason being, one party will be pursued by another for whatever reason and the significant other of this certain party will not only be able to see what is happening but will attempt to tell the pursued party that this is in fact happening. What will often happen then is the pursued party will try and downplay the pursuit, arguing that the pursuit is non-existent or that the pursuer is just being nice. What should be known and what is widely known but often overlooked is the fact that people use niceness and sympathy to manipulate others into doing many things. A situation such as this can resemble infidelity because at a certain age in life, people are generally expected to know better. They are expected to be able to weed out deception and deceptive practices. When certain people are not able to see something as easily as someone else, say for instance, the games that his or her significant other is playing, that person will be thought of as gullible, stupid, naïve, dimwitted and whatever else. In addition to these thoughts, the significant other who is proficient at sniffing out this type of trickery will or may think that his significant other will be too gullible, naïve, dimwitted and whatever else to circumvent a possible liaison in the future.

Every action in this world has a reaction or a result. People's actions are normally dictated by three things; 1) the fact that they know and are working toward the outcome of their actions. 2) The fact that they are totally unaware of the potential or actual outcome of their actions. 3) The fact that they just don't give a damn about the outcome of their actions. Number two is the main reason people find themselves in trouble or if not in trouble, then in sticky situations. A person with a good heart may give a prostitute a ride home if she were just robbed and left standing outside naked. A jealous or insecure significant other after seeing or hearing this, may assume that there is more to the story than what actually exists. Nosey neighbors and friends often contribute to the belief of infidelity by adding their two cents where it doesn't belong. The <u>thought</u> of infidelity is the biggest enemy to a relationship. This is why trust is paramount. There are no two ways about it, if you are in a relationship, you either trust your partner or you don't. There is no such thing as complete trust. There is no such thing as a little bit of trust either. There is however what's known as satisfactory trust. This is the comforting level of 'I'm secure in what you tell me.' There is also always the possibility that 'you may use my trust in you to support your own twisted agenda but I will refuse to believe that.' If there's doubt, even the slightest bit, the relationship can be in jeopardy. In conclusion, it must be stated that many situations in this world can be looked at two ways; the truth and a front to dissuade someone from the truth. A front to dissuade someone from the truth is self-explanatory but the truth, the tricky, stranger than fiction truth, is often a situation, which resembles infidelity.

Chapter Ten
Money And Sex – The Great Definitives

Sex, the foundation of a great many relationships - It is this one passion, which has the power to determine how long some relationships last and how some others are financed. Sex applies to a relationship in many ways. For some people there is the pursuit. For others there is control or the manipulation - that is using of sex to get his or her way. There are still others who use sex for recreation and those who only use it for procreation. For certain people, the pursuit of sexual intercourse is the sole motivation behind them even considering a relationship. This is not rocket science. These people will make achieving the plateau of physical intimacy their goal and being that goals are not usually continual, once these people attain that satisfaction, they will care about little else in the relationship. This is also not rocket science. Almost everybody who is in a relationship or who has been in a relationship has had the experience of witnessing a person act one way then act completely different after the sex act has been fulfilled. This is a bad thing but would not be if people would just discuss their goals and agendas ahead of time. However, people do anything in life to achieve certain goals and one of the biggest things they do to achieve the goal of sexual satisfaction is lie. There are some continual goals such as a happy and productive relationship or raising children into happy and productive adults but these types of goals are usually reserved for those who actually desire a relationship in the first place. Pursuing sex is like any other pursuit in life. There are potential advantages and potential disadvantages to achieving the prize. The most motivating factor however is the belief that the potential advantages will outweigh the potential bad. Many people for instance believe that good or great sex will bring about a good or great relationship. Sometimes they even feel that an extremely high level of ecstasy will change a person's mind into desiring a relationship if that thought was never in the person's mind to begin with. The desire for a relationship can barely hold a candle to the desire for physical intimacy when it comes to certain individuals. The reason for this is most often because of the depressing attachments, which tag along in relationships. To certain people, sex is the best feeling and most important thing in the world. Many people who don't fully understand the ramifications of commitment only want happy times and good feelings during their relationships. Since it is impossible to have a physical, intimate relationship every single day, those who maintain that belief are destined to meet up with problems. To avoid the inevitable relationship problems that almost all couples face, these certain individuals will only stay for the good times or only come by when the propensity for intimate physical contact is at its highest point (like Friday nights when the desired individual is under the influence or when the desired individual's significant other is not home.) The desire for sex is one of the strongest desires in the world. People will pay for it, they will mentally and physically coerce others into indulging in it and a few horny, demented individuals will even kill for it. Many in relationships understand and agree that sex is an important part of the union. However they do not always understand or agree how important sex actually is to their partner. The demand for sex is often underrated – so much so that people, for some strange reason feel that their interest in sex is or must be equivalent to their partners. These people feel that if sex on a bi-weekly basis is sufficient for them, then it should be just as sufficient for the husband or wife. Not to beat a dead horse but lack of communication causes these types of problems, whereas honest and effective communication is what will eradicate or at least alleviate them.

Communication must be in place before relationships are consummated. That way there will be no mid relationship surprises.

People use sex as a means of control. This is not a new practice; it is a method of manipulation, which has been around I believe for centuries. People use this manipulation method by dangling the prospect of intercourse in front of someone the same way a cruel hearted individual would dangle a $100 bill in front of a homeless person. The level of need or level of greed exuded by the homeless individual would dictate what that homeless person would be willing to do. The same thing holds true for people driven by passion.

As long as these people 'think' the possibility of intimacy exists – no matter how small or miniscule it may be; these people will continue to be subservient to the ones they are interested in. This is one of the ways in which many mismatched couples get together. A man who is not considered 'handsome' by society's standards may have his sights set on a woman who is considered beauty pageant winning material. Even though the woman has no intention whatsoever on becoming in any way intimate with this man, as long as he believes there is the remote possibility of a roll in the hay, he will continue to do for her anything, which he believes will increase his chances. The woman at this point assumes the role of the person in the previous example holding the $100 bill. She can have this man pay rent, car notes, mortgage installments, whatever – until she either gets tired of using him, has sex with him or until he has sex with somebody who captures his interest more than her.

There are many advantages when it comes to having sex. One of the advantages of achieving one's goal in the pursuit of sexual intercourse includes the fulfillment of knowing that you have achieved a goal that you have set for yourself. Many people rarely reach all of the goals they set for themselves, whether those goals are financial, as in earning a million dollars before the age of thirty – or family oriented, as in purchasing a home to be able to leave to children and future generations or personal, as in having sex with the most popular person in school. Consummating a relationship with someone is believed to be the deepest level of affection. It is believed that once physical intimacies are shared, the feelings of like and attraction are instantly transformed into those of love. This belief can be advantageous for someone who really doesn't care about another but who wants to give the impression that he or she does.

Another advantage is the removal of the early relationship uneasiness, which many couples experience in the first few weeks or months of a relationship. People are often unsure of when to discuss the idea of sexual relations, if it is not done on the first day or discussed before a relationship is undertaken. The fact that couples see each other naked and engage in sexual activity removes the stresses and fears of 'Does he or she really like me?' After sex is in place, there is often the feeling of 'Good, now that sex is out of the way, we can get down to the real relationship.' The physical relations stage is usually the ending of the probationary period in most relationships.

There are several disadvantages to having sex as well. Some of the disadvantages of achieving one's goal in the pursuit of sexual intercourse include competition and pregnancy. Healthy competition is enjoyed by siblings, members of sports teams and by members of opposing companies. On the relationship front however, competition can be dangerous. Those competing for intercourse will cause each individual in the race to try and out do the other. This can be accomplished by the political approach of character assassination, which is the same as making the opponent seem as unfit as possible – to wit; mentioning things he or she has done or is doing. It could also be accomplished by the approach of certain governmental agencies as in eliminating the competition, literally. It may even be accomplished by the simplistic approach of many second and third graders, lying. Competition is sometimes a disadvantage because whatever the opponent says or does is something that you will have to say or do better. If you know in your heart that you cannot out do them and your interest in this person is only physical, chances are you will lie. As with most lies, they will need to be continually enhanced to achieve the desired goal. If you achieve your goal of intimacy with someone, often it will be the same as being ranked number one at a particular sport, someone will always be trying to take your title or as with relationships, trying to take your piece of booty. If this person is in fact only a piece of booty, chances are you will not care one way or the other if someone treads on your territory. However, many times when a couple has sexual relations, one person in that couple gets whipped, meaning the sex is so good to them that they will do whatever necessary to keep the flow coming. Now picture that for a second, you have sex with somebody whom you really don't care about, they become captivated by your loving and become like a barnacle to a ship. Somebody else, who does have actual interest in this barnacle type person, continues to press the issue with him or her to get involved. The barnacle type person confides in you and expects you to confront the other and let him or her know that the two of you are a couple. When you hesitate or refuse, the barnacle type person begins to feel used and/or discarded and then plots to kill you or some crazy shit like that; all because your competition would not leave well enough alone and respect the fact that their target of interest had no interest in them.

Another disadvantage in achieving one's goal of sexual intercourse is the possibility of pregnancy. Pregnancy is the major occupational hazard of infidelity or sex in general and although there are many people who want each sexual encounter to result in pregnancy, there are many more who don't. The wonderful and at the same time disgustingly pitiful thing about this world is the fact that everyone has what is called free will. That is the free will to do whatever they want, whether it's be an asshole or be a saint or be aggressive as opposed to passive. That free will extends to having the capability to lie or not. When people pursue others just for sex, nine times out of ten, they are visually stimulated and motivated. They see what they want and they go after it. Few times do they actually know the mindset of the person they're pursuing and even fewer are the times they actually know what type of plan this person may already have for you in his or her life. Some of these people who are being pursued may want to have sex and nothing else, some of them may want to have sex and a relationship, some of them may want to have sex, a relationship and a child. The bad part about free will and lying is that a person may combine the two, use their free will to lie and get pregnant, thereby creating absolute hell from the child support enforcement team for the dummy who got them that way. (And I can use the name dummy because that's what happened to me!) Pregnancy, or the using of, in regards to women can happen a number of ways. A woman can swear up and down, left to right that she does not want to have children. She may have all types of protection available, from birth control pills to a year's supply of condoms hidden in her closet. If due to fate or John Q. Murphy and his law, that woman gets pregnant, she could and more than likely will have a change of heart and instantly desire to keep the child. Go figure. There are many trifling women, as described above, who have intentions on getting pregnant all along but will lie and then act surprised when they turn up that way – you know the old 'I didn't think I could get pregnant but now that we have this miracle baby, let's be thankful and raise him or her in a mutually supportive and equally jubilant environment.' Then there are those who have been hurt as described above by the barnacle type people. These women let their emotions run away or get involved in sexual relationships prematurely, without completely understanding what level of interest their partner actually has. These women will fall in love with someone who does not love them – right up until the point when they are bitch slapped with a reality stick – after which they will become hateful, looking to exact their revenge on the first man who gives them the time of day. Women will do this (get pregnant) because they want unquestionable revenge or because they feel it's the only way they can keep a man in their lives.

Pregnancy, in regards to men, is a definite disadvantage when it comes to achieving one's goal of sexual intercourse. This is a disadvantage because although many men are visually stimulated and desire sex quicker and more often than women, these men do not nearly as much desire the prospect of being dads. This is also disadvantageous because men have no say so in the matter of pregnancy other than 'can he or she have my last name?' If you do not know this, let me be the first to tell you, the child support system is almost entirely for the woman. If you father a child and you work and you don't pay the required support, believe me you're gonna pay. You may pay a little, you may pay a lot but you're gonna pay! Achieving one's goal of sexual intercourse can put a person at a disadvantage financially if they are in a relationship and they get the person they're cheating with pregnant. In a situation such as this, many times the man will want to keep the child as well as the affair hidden. This can wipe out a man's finances because he will have to pay an undetermined amount of 'hush money' to the mother of his illegitimate child. This can also backfire because some men will instantly pay to keep the woman quiet, not knowing if the child is in fact his own. Women can capitalize on this intimidation factor if the child even remotely looks like the man in question and is the approximate age of a child who would have resulted from a liaison whenever that liaison took place. All that needs to be said is I'm having or I have your child, I need money every month or I'm telling your wife. Since most men don't want to lose what they have at home, they will send that monetary gift every month without question. Here's a bit of wisdom for you sex addicts or should I say those of you who only want sex and nothing else; don't have sex with anyone you don't wanna marry – trust me, that orgasm will come back to bite you in the ass!

People say that there are only two insatiable desires in this world. The first one is sex, the other is money. I do not believe there is any substantial love of one above the other because for every horny, perverted, sexual deviant in this world, there is more than likely some money hungry, gold diggin' user to match. Money and sex, like the title of this chapter states, are definitive – they are the bottom line, as far as what many people are looking for when it comes to relationships. They are the things people manipulate others for. They are the things people kill others for. In a world where people are judged by the materialistic, the greedy and those that have, the have nots are often forgotten or dismissed for not having any value. In modern society, the job a person has determines his or her self worth. If a person has an executive position in a well-publicized company, that person is thought of as well off. If a person works as a security officer, quite often that person is thought of as having no money, no education and little ambition – and I speak from personal experience. The mindset of this society is so irreparably damaged that if a particular person has a new car, the general consensus is that that particular person has money. If a person has on new clothes, after not changing his or her wardrobe for a while, again, that person must have achieved some increased level of financial being. People have become so conditioned into believing the privilege of having money will not be completely enjoyable unless there is someone around to show it off to. (Don't know about that one) To go to the basics, money is anything that is generally accepted by people in exchange for the things they sell or the work they do. In other words, it is a medium of exchange. The opposite of this is what's called a barter system – where one person would have to trade what they have to get what they want from someone else. The barter system is what many relationships today are based on. Some in relationships say 'I don't have time to do this for or with you, so I'll do this instead.' This can be sex, housework or any other recreational activity. This type of barter comes into play because people don't have time or do not desire to make time for others in their circle. Too often people make money the main focus of their lives. They feel if they do not have money or enough money, then life is not worth living. In families where both adults work full time, the bills are often satisfied but the social life tends to suffer. Children of these parents suffer too. They become children of babysitters and children of relatives, rarely getting to know their own parents. These types of children are often spoiled with lavish items as a way of excusing the parents' all too often absences but what many of these parents do not realize is that children need time more than anything else. Money is great. It allows people to enjoy life. The more money one has, consequently the more that person will be able to enjoy many of the things life has to offer but money is also believed to be evil. In fact it has been called the root of all evil. This stems from the belief that mismanaged money or an excessive amount will only lead to bad things. Money itself is not evil. Money is little more than paper, silver and copper currency. It is the people who possess it and make the decisions with it who are evil. Money does not define a person. A person's actions with money is what defines them. If a person wins the lottery for twenty million dollars and another person plays the stock market and acquires twenty million dollars, who is smarter? Neither. Timing can sometimes be the reason why people make millions or make zip. Both of the above described individuals can be viewed as smart and or lucky. If one was to blow it all however, that person would be looked at as an asshole. If however, either one were to invest those funds and possibly double or triple that twenty million, he or she would be looked at as wise. It would not matter one way or another how they acquired it. It's what a person does with what they have that counts. There is this belief among many that a person who has little available funds is insignificant when compared to a person who has a million dollar 401k. This belief will not change. This belief is about the same as a voluptuous woman being a more satisfying sex partner than someone who is not so 'well rounded.' This belief only caters to the specific desires of an individual. People have their own circles of influence. They have their own likes and dislikes based own their own experiences and observations. Many weightlifters for example believe they are better than skinny people just because they are bigger. Many rich people believe they are better than non rich people just because they are rich. The same thing holds true for the belief about voluptuous women. There are marriages based on money or should I say the pursuit of, there are lottery scams, insurance scams and basically scams of every size shape and description - all for the pursuit of money. The pursuit of money is a necessity in today's world, unlike the pursuit of sex. Money is a necessity people cannot do without. Sex on the other hand is a desired luxury. Now it should be stated that if everybody were to stop having sex, in a hundred years or so this world would most likely cease to exist. So in a sense, sex is a necessity also but the sex I'm referring to is the procreation kind as opposed to the recreation kind. Those who do not engage in sex are not that much different than those of us who do. There are many virgins in this world who hold good jobs, participate in many extra curricular activities and who are just generally productive members of society. Unsurprisingly, people who make sex the main focal point of their lives, meaning those who have sex the way most other people work regular jobs, with the exception of prostitutes, pimps and those in the sex industry are usually not as well off.

There are plenty of advantages and disadvantages, which come with money. The advantages, we see all too often - such as the expensive cars, the overpriced homes and the exploitation of beautiful women. The desire for expensive cars is often understandable. Almost everybody has a dream car – a car, which has every feature under the sun and is little more than $200,000 away. That's why they call it a 'dream' car. The home is also understandable because almost everyone desires the amount of space, which would facilitate close friends and family but women are starting to give much too much credibility to the 'everybody has a price' thing. One of the disadvantages to having money or should I say wealth, is that you instantly become a point of interest for those who don't. That point of interest can stretch from entrepreneurs seeking to learn your business secrets to start up companies seeking financing to the average Joe seeking a handout. There are philanthropists who make a habit out of giving money to charitable organizations and well deserving folks but the bad thing about that is sooner or later, if a person continues to give, eventually their giving capabilities will run out. When someone has money, it's hard to know which other people really need and which other people really want, when it comes to funding. Just ask anyone who has hit the lottery, once they do, everybody and their mother will seemingly come around seeking money to help with their problems. This puts the person with money in kind of an awkward situation. If they give to everybody who asks, as stated before, soon they will be broke. If they refuse the wrong individual, that individual may resort to rash measures to acquire some of the rich person's money – and the belief will most likely be 'they're rich, they ain't gonna miss it.' This is awkward because when you think about it, you're like 'what do you do?' This is dangerous because the most popular rash method is the abducting of family.

The disadvantages to having money are different according to gender. For men
and this is not entirely a disadvantage, often the belief will be 'he worked hard, saved his money and probably sold stock.' For women, the belief will likely be 'she worked hard under a man, saved her money and probably sold ass. The belief is that men are historically smarter than women.

That's funny though because historically women believe they are smarter than men. Going back to the example about women being exploited, I have a question; why is it that when a man makes a few million dollars, women who otherwise would never sit next to this man on a bus, now want to sit in his car? Is it that that man is exploiting that woman or is it that she is exploiting herself? Hmmm. The bottom line here is that some people will do **anything** to acquire money. Money has power. Money is power. Money is magical. It makes ugly people handsome and pretty, the same way alcohol does at closing time.

Chapter Eleven
Friends With Benefits

I know some of you cheating asses turned to this chapter first. It's okay, I'm not mad at you. The concept behind the title of this chapter, 'Friends With Benefits' is wildly popular in today's society. It is so popular because everybody either has a friend with whom they are receiving benefits from or they know of someone who is receiving benefits from another. Most of us understand that the 'friends with benefits' title is nothing more than a clever way of saying 'this person is a friend of mine, with whom, on occasion, I have sex.' There are some people however who do not understand that the term 'benefits' is not the same as it is for people on public assistance. It does not; in most instances refer to a 'trick' or someone who will buy a person everything they want in return for sexual favors. Having a friend with benefits is not cheating unless you or this person is married. The term friends with benefits should not be taken out of context – it is cheating, but only when applied to relationships. By itself, a friend with benefits is not a form of infidelity but basically a promiscuous, non - committed union. The friend with benefits is the proverbial 'stand by' lover – on call for emergencies or for periods of relationship unemployment. Unemployment is the period when a person is between jobs. Relationship unemployment is the period when a person is between relationships. The friend with benefits is basically the equivalent of an 'off the books' job used to tide someone over until another main job kicks in. The off the books job still provides the main resource, which is usually money but it will rarely provide anything else such as health benefits, retirement benefits or sick/personal time. It is just there as a band – aid; a temporary fix. The friend with benefits type of unification is preferred for several reasons. First, there is the understanding between both parties that there is no relationship in the traditional sense between the two. This means that either party can go out and sleep with as many people as he or she pleases. There is no commitment or condition of exclusiveness. In addition to each party being able to sleep around until their heart's content, the belief is in place that either of them can abort the union at will and restart it as necessary – and both without any negative ramifications. This type of agreement is also preferred because the friend, nine times out of ten is an actual friend, someone that the other party knows more than just intimately. This in itself is a benefit. There is no having to date somebody new, no going through the awkward phase of getting to know and deciding if this person is worthy enough to have sex with you. With a friend, chances are you already know his or her good and bad points. Most times, you have a pretty decent picture of their sexual habits or history. Friends alleviate much of the worry, which comes along with someone you don't know.

Another benefit of the friends with benefits situation is the peace of mind, which comes from knowing that both mindsets are the same or closely related. There is no 'I want a baby' down the road or 'I want you to stop seeing other people.' Usually friends with benefits are just that – one friend with the benefit of non committal sex. Even though the freedom to be promiscuous exists in friends with benefits type situations, most people keep the relationship just between the three. (The husband, the wife & the natural partner) Benefit relationships offer a comfortable environment to express one's sexuality. There is little worry of sexually transmitted diseases and no relationship attachments, as in let's go shopping or let's go visit my parents or even let's walk down the street hand in hand. In this type of relationship, there is affection but it is never publicized. People on the street will almost never be able to tell that sex is being had between the two unless one of the two blabs. People who enjoy this type of union, can proclaim they have their cake and are able to eat it too. 'A friend who has sex and without commitment' – the concept seems almost unimaginable. A friends with benefits union, by most accounts, is the perfect relationship. However, as with most good things in life, there is always a potential down side. The down side to a friends with benefits union is the one thing every player, playette, playboy or person who just desires a casual and physical relationship fears – and that is commitment. Sex has power and no, I'm not just talking about the power of the p-u-s-s-y. I'm talking about the power to disillusion. Sex, especially good sex, will make a person believe that they are 'appreciated' more than they actually are. The reason this happens is because sex has a lot to do with feelings. People who say they have sex without feelings are lying. There is of course the physical feeling associated with the act of intercourse but more so is the emotional attachment, which comes along after. People cannot escape these two. What many of them do however is put aside their feelings as if they were dirty laundry. A person can hide, put aside or just ignore the feelings, which come along with sex for a long time but because a person is good at covering feelings does not mean they are good at eradicating them. To every side, there is an opposite and to every rule, there is an exception. Some people who get involved in the 'benefits' situation are not always as strong as the other party in that relationship. These people have sex and from that day, garner an attraction, which would make Romeo and Juliet pale in comparison. These people enjoy the sex so much that they feel 1) their partners must have enjoyed it just as much and 2) a relationship is sure or soon to follow. The widely accepted term for this ailment is called 'being whipped.' Being whipped is what causes miscommunication. It causes people to forget any verbal, written or implied agreement, quickly. Relationships, which start off as friends, then gravitate into the benefits category are often seen by one party as progression. That party, man or woman may be under the impression that because the sex is good and the friendship is intact, a committed, lifelong relationship is inevitable. Silly them! Miscommunication of this type will always cause hurt feelings. It can cause a person to feel as if they are being used and the only reason or main reason this happens is because people do not stay true to their original agendas. I've seen it happen more times than I prefer to count. A person will plan to have sex with another, with the understanding that the interaction will be nothing more than a physical liaison every now and then. (In other words, weekend stimulation) The condoms are bought, the birth control pills are standing valiantly by the side of the bed and the euphoric feeling of 'I'm gonna get me some non committal sex!' clouds the air. The couple has sex and to one, it's the best he or she has ever had. The other however, deems the act as routine. Historically men hold the crown when it comes to being stalkers after good sex, even though women are historically known for their emotions. Let's say in this particular case, the woman gets so wrapped up in the fact that the man was the only one able to make her have an orgasm, that the next time they do it, she conveniently forgets the 'in place' agreement and begins to act like someone who is whipped. She will try and deceive, coerce or buy this man into a relationship. The deceit can be her knowingly, administering a broken condom to her partner before they have sex. The coercion can be her setting up a hidden video camera, enacting a 'fantasy' rape scene and then using that against her lover.

The buying of a relationship is the most fun and is what takes a very strong, moral fortitude to resist. A person who wants somebody who they know can and will provide good sex is not above buying that person a car, paying that person's rent or pulling that person from the dire straits, which is their financial life. The person who just wanted sex without commitment, now has the option to take the gifts and risk leading the other person on and being labeled a user or refusing the gifts, thereby potentially confusing the other person. See, what a person will do is buy or offer another person something, and then when that other person accepts, the one who bought that particular something will feel as if they are automatically owed something. People don't do things just to be nice anymore; there is almost always an ulterior motive. Just in case there is any confusion, I'll use my favorite example people, Tasha and Ryan. Let's say Tasha likes Ryan. Ryan however just wants to boink Tasha. Ryan boinks Tasha so well that afterwards Tasha feels compelled to offer, buy or give Ryan whatever he wants – the sky is the limit. This is understandable, Ryan provides Tasha with good feeling, so Tasha wants to reciprocate those good feelings to Ryan. What is not completely understandable or good is that if Ryan accepts even one of the proposed gifts, the belief will be – 'I bought you this, now you owe me something!' the 'this' can be a car, payment of bills or any number of things, which can lead up to a relationship. The acceptance of any of those things is what will often mislead another into believing that there is an implied relationship. A person does not always have to say 'will you be my boyfriend or girlfriend' and receive a yes or no to feel as if he or she is in a relationship. Sometimes if a person buys you a car, you are instantly indebted to that person – whether you accept that indebtedness or not. Next scenario – let's say Tasha and Ryan had gotten together in the same manner as stated above and Tasha offered to get Ryan anything he desired and Ryan was to say no, Tasha quite possibly could become confused as to the actual attraction or interest level held by Ryan. Sex has that type of power. The bottom line in a friends with benefits situation, just like in any other type of successful relationship is that there must be communication. It must be clear and it must be ongoing. Sex without communication is fun – oh boy is it fun! But it is best had between prostitute and john. (Hypothetically of course!) Unspoken words and feelings often lead to assumptions. Assumptions have always and will always lead to trouble.

Some friends with benefits relationships last a few weeks, some last a few months and yes, some even last a few years. The longer they last, the more potential there is for misunderstanding. The friend with benefits relations, which go on for years, often break up and rekindle. This is the cooling off period while one of the parties is in an actual committed relationship with someone else. If that actual committed relationship goes awry, then the friends with benefits union may kick back in and the union may kick back in for any number of reasons, such as the inability by one partner to be alone after being in a relationship for so long or the inability to continue the amount of physical intimacy, which was shared while he or she was involved. The misunderstanding can come about by one person in the friends with benefits union thinking the rekindling of that type of union is an actual kindling of feelings. The one thing about this world, which cannot be disputed, is the fact that nothing lasts forever. This applies especially to feelings, as well as the rules put in place to dictate how they should be manipulated. People can agree to have sex with each other as long as they are both consenting and not in a relationship with anyone else for as long as possible but the one thing many of these people don't take into account is the overpowering effects of time. Time causes change in all aspects of life – especially in relationships. The longer a couple is together, the more its feelings toward each other will solidify. You can tell a heart not to like someone a thousand times but that does not mean the heart will listen.

Another potential downside of a friends with benefits union is gaining the acceptance that you and this person may forever be just friends. People want the whole package, when it comes to relationships. They want the three b's – beauty, brains and body. Unfortunately as life often dictates, it is impossible to find everything, which is often desired, in one person. It is possible however to find a certain number of things in one person that no other person can match. These things for example, could be high intellect, supermodel body, great cook, excellent parental figure and/or porn star sex. For a certain person, some of these attributes could be all that is necessary to sustain a relationship. The bad part about this could be that the person with the high intellect and supermodel body only likes to have sex once a month or maybe this person likes to have sex everyday but not with you because you are what's considered a 'friend.'

Chapter Twelve
Violations, Misdemeanors and Felonies

There are certain laws, which govern life, as well as laws, which govern the world in which we live. Some of the laws, which govern life, are the law of gravity, the law of relativity and the law of physics. Some of the laws, which govern the world in which we presently live, are those dealing with church and state. Punishment for breaking some of these laws, vary from jail time to afterlife punishment. The charges for breaking these laws are divided into three main parts. They are violations, misdemeanors and felonies.

A violation of a law is usually the least serious. Using the laws in New York State for example, punishment for a violation does not require any jail time. The charges are usually either settled by a monetary fine or dismissed. Violations can be anything from spitting to jaywalking. In regards to a relationship, the punishment for the violation charge is similar. A violation in a relationship is something classified as not so serious - something, which would require maybe a slap on the wrist or a stern warning as punishment. Being in the presence of one's significant other and ogling another would be considered a violation. Flirting would also be viewed as one of the lesser serious crimes. In relationships, there will always be things one party does, which will perturb, disturb or just piss the hell off the other person. A person's understanding or willingness to forgive is what classifies an infraction into the violation, misdemeanor or felony category. A person in a relationship who spends an undue amount of time with his or her ex can be viewed as a violation, misdemeanor or felony depending on the circumstances. Most relationships today are not new and by new I'm referring to both parties being the only one each other has dated. Most people in relationships have a past and that past usually includes kids as well as several members of the opposite sex. Married couples far too often break up and get involved with other people. The people they get involved with may not always be able to understand that the ex husband or wife will always be a part of their life – especially if the kids are not with them. Some people will believe that if a person who spends time with his or her kids, has to pacify the parent of the kids in order to do so, then they are doing so in an attempt to rekindle the relationship they had with that parent in the beginning. There are situations where the custodial parent is an absolute dick and the non custodial parent has to be even nicer than he normally is to see the child. This does not mean that love or lust is present. This means a person must do what needs to be done to achieve the desired goal.

A misdemeanor is the next step on the ladder of intensity when it comes to the seriousness of crimes. Misdemeanors are crimes, which can land a person in jail for up to a year, as well as require that person to pay a financial penalty. Misdemeanors can be drug possession, disorderly conduct and/or the possession of certain weapons. In regards to a relationship, misdemeanors can be anything from you or your significant other receiving hang up calls to you getting caught in an unhelpful lie. Remember the difference, helpful lie – 'yes dear, anything you wear looks great and if it doesn't it's the manufacturers fault.' Unhelpful lie – 'that girl you saw me with was my cousin, I just don't know her phone number or address.' As far as the hang up calls, people will make mistakes from now until the end of time. These people may mistakenly dial your number and hang up in your significant others face when they realize their mistake. People may accidentally hit the flash button at the exact moment your significant other answers the phone. In some rare instances, the person you are being natural with may call to speak to you and may hang up if your husband or wife picks up the phone. All three of the previous examples are viable scenarios, which could be why a hang up call is received. Nine times out of ten, if you live with your significant other or they pick up your cell phone, which scenario are they most likely to believe? Right, number three. The bottom line is that there needs to be trust. Whether the relationship is a violation, misdemeanor or felony, how much you trust this person will definitely be a factor.

A felony is the most serious degree of crime that can be committed. Felonies are crimes, which usually land a person in jail for more than one year all the way up to life in prison. Murder, kidnapping and arson are some examples of popular felonies, which can put a person away for life. There are different types of felonies, class a, class b and so on and so forth. Possessing a gun or a certain amount of drugs are also automatic felonies. In regards to relationships, a felony is usually one thing, infidelity. People feel that infidelity is the emotional equivalent of murder. It is something, which if certain people had their way, would subject the offender to at the very least, a lengthy prison term. Although infidelity, unlike felonies in the criminal justice system, is able to be forgiven, people hold it in such high regard that often they hold the infraction over a person's head for years. Cheating to some people is unforgivable. It is seen as the highest form of disrespect and to some people, there is no retribution. A person who has been cheated on may not be able to inflict physical lifelong punishment but often times the mental and emotional withdrawal by that person may cause their partner more harm than an actual jail cell. Unlike the felonies in the criminal justice system, infidelity only has one level. There is no class a or b felony in regards to cheating. There is what some like to call emotional cheating but that, in my opinion is a very long stretch of the imagination. Cheating is a physical act. Cheating on any other level is more or less a fantasy until you act on it.

Somebody in a relationship talking about or looking at the anatomy of another can be forgotten as easily as a dropped penny in a check cashing place. This type of relationship violation is easily forgivable due to the fact that talking about a person's anatomy can be positive or negative – meaning they can say that person has an ugly or attractive shape. The person in a relationship, who looks at another, while in the presence of his or her significant other can say they were only looking at that person because he or she repulses them. This may or may not be the actual truth. If a male walks with his wife and notices a female, who he deems gorgeous, he can sneak a peek by saying she's ugly or she's dressed inappropriately. If all the male wanted to do was get a peek at the other woman without getting smacked or involved in an argument, he will more than likely accomplish his goal. If there are others in relationships who do this without going through the trouble of trying to cover it up, their partners may easily overlook it because chances are their partners will understand that there are many beautiful people in this world who are deserving of a second glance but these partners are more than likely going to desire the same courtesy when they observe somebody who tweaks their interest.

A relationship misdemeanor, such as staying out all night without calling can cause speculation but that speculation will not be long lasting either, depending upon the level of trust. If the perpetrator of the 'all night out without calling' infraction has no priors, meaning no prior bouts of infidelity, where he or she had been caught, chances are the significant other may eventually forget about it and forgive them. If the perpetrator has had a prior affair or unresolved situation, which resembled an affair, that misdemeanor can quickly jump into the felony classification. Something such as staying out all night violates one of the unwritten laws of most relationships. Daybreak is the invisible line, which invites or prevents an argument when a person in a committed relationship goes out alone. Other relationship misdemeanors include keeping secrets that a partner is aware of but whose content remains hidden. Nobody's life is an open book and nobody's life should be. Everyone in this world has at least one thing they want to conceal from the general public as well as from the person they are involved with – however in a relationship, the greater the amount of concealment, the more room exists for suspicion. A productive relationship should at the very least have open communication between both parties. Someone keeping a secret or secrets can be seen as a lack of communication. Secrets cause a person to invent mental scenarios. If a person knows a secret is being kept by his or her partner but does not know the secret or know why the secret is being kept, that person will begin to wonder. The wonder will not be for the good because secrets, with the exception of surprises and/or surprise parties are usually negative. A secret would be classified as a misdemeanor due to its annoying but potentially damaging nature. It can also be on the level of a violation as in 'she's not a real blonde' or it can have the potential to become a felony. What propels the intensity of a secrets' power is the ability of the person it is being kept from to dismiss it or not.

Relationship felonies, such as being natural, can cause irreparable damage to some people because they deal with the heart. A felony of this type can cause homicides, suicides and in some instances, both. It must be understood that while being natural is considered a relationship ending violation to some people, it is considered a sport to others. From the time people are very young, misinterpretations about the intensity of infidelity exist. Some people think 'hey everybody does it' while others believe if a person does it, he or she should be killed or at least castrated. Lack of communication or miscommunication causes these types of people to get together and sometimes, the end result is what was described above. People who violate this felony relationship law like to have it all. They like to have their cake and eat it too, so to speak - but what they do not like is when the tables are turned on them. Nine times out of ten, a person who cheats on his or her significant other or who is promiscuous with no intention of settling down, will be distraught, heartbroken and just genuinely hurt, if they find out their significant other is doing the same thing to them. People love to cheat but they almost never take into account their partner's feelings while doing so. This 'smack' into reality will cause a person to either stop cheating or cheat more aggressively. The big belief is that a person who cheats often or who is just genuinely promiscuous has no heart. People also believe that this type of person will never garner an attraction to anyone, thereby making it easier for that type of person to continue cheating. What some people fail to realize is that the longer people are around others, they garner an attraction, sometimes whether they want to or not. These people do have hearts, they just also have problems. The interpretation or the manipulation of the interpretation of certain laws is one of the things, that can help people facing punishment. That's why lawyers were invented. Depending upon the circumstances, set punishment for violations of these laws can be amended or eluded. When a person has been or is being natural, there are always circumstances, which caused the indiscretion. Before someone is ostracized for cheating, it is often a good idea to examine which factors led up to the action. Many times, the reason for the affair is much more than inadequate control of hormones or lack of emotional fulfillment.

There is another type of felony, which is to some, on the same penalty level as infidelity. It is the crime of physical abuse. Physical abuse is punching, smacking, kicking or any related method of encouragement. For those of you who may not know, this type of behavior is wrong and has no place in a relationship. Physical abuse is a loss of control. It is not an alternative to rational discussion as many people like to believe. The one similarity between this unwritten relationship law and the criminal law is that this one will send a person to jail. The loss of control, which leads to physical abuse, can be attributed to many things, for instance stress. Stress often gets the blame for depression, mood swings and a whole host of other ailments but by itself, it does not cause a person to beat up on his or her significant other. A hard day at work will rarely cause someone to say 'I'm gonna go home and punch my wife in the mouth.' A combination of stresses, on the other hand, is often what drives a person off the trail of tranquility. A person could have just lost their job on Monday, received an eviction notice on Tuesday, had their car stolen on Wednesday and a fire in their apartment on Thursday – and to top it off, this person's significant other wants to start a fight by blaming the cause of the fire on the other party. This is what one would call a combination of stresses. People go through scenarios, such as this quite often. If this were more than just a hypothetical example, then the idea of choking the living shit out of a nagging husband or wife could possibly be understood. <u>It would in no way be justified but definitely understood.</u>

In conclusion, the only true way to know if someone you care about is cheating on you is by playing big brother. Follow them. Use audio/video surveillance, binoculars, sexy decoys – whatever. When it comes to protecting one's heart, there is no price too high. Some people make an actual job out of cheating. To catch these people, you must make it more than a job; you must make it an actual science. Listening to one's heart is helpful. Listening to one's friends is also helpful. Paying attention to one's conscience may be the most helpful of all but the assistance of all three will not equal clear and undisputable evidence. Catching your husband leaving a woman's house does not necessarily mean they've just finished screwing. It could mean that they are friends and you do not understand enough to accept that type of friendship, which they share. The woman's home, from which the husband is spotted leaving, could be owned by somebody that the husband and wife both used to be friends with but now for some reason or another, the wife hates. The husband may still be friends with this woman and can only associate freely with her at her home. Finding your best friend's number in your wife's cell phone does not mean something negative is going on. Because you know in your heart that your best friend is the most promiscuous person you know outside of yourself, does not mean he has his sights set on your lady. The two of them could be planning a surprise party for you and may need to confer with each other while apart. Granted, these explanations are extreme possibilities, maybe even the most extreme on the extreme spectrum but the possibility exists that they are still possible. Situations such as these can be nothing more than those, which resemble infidelity. Because these situations exist does not mean that your significant other is not cheating either, it just means a situation exists, which needs clarification. The last thing you want to do is ruin an otherwise 'good' relationship because of silly, unfounded accusations. If you suspect your significant other of cheating and not because you found this book lying around the house but because you actually believe you have a legitimate reason, then hire a private investigator, play private investigator yourself and gather evidence or send in the decoys. Whatever you do never, never and let me say this again; never assume they're cheating! For those of you who don't know, when you assume, you generally make an ass out of u and me.

If on the other hand, you have attained that level of acceptance where you realize that everybody in this world is human and capable of mistakes and you want to prepare yourself for the possibility of infidelity, then what needs to happen is a flat out, honest conversation about the ifs, what ifs, possibilities and potential accidents. (Potential accidents being if a person was too inebriated to realize what they were doing.) In other words, if you get together with someone and are a little unsure but not yet financially stable enough for the prenuptial, then sit the other person down and ask; if either of us cheats and gets caught or cheats and decides our conscience is not strong enough to hide the indiscretion, what are we gonna do? Are we going to stay together and attempt to work it out or will the first indiscretion be the last? If a child is conceived because of an adulterous liaison, how will we handle that potential iota of adversity? Questions, such as these and others related to them will alleviate many of the potential problems, which are sure to arise in most relationships. However, one may need to ask themselves; is this providing me with the level of comfort, which will help me co exist peacefully with my significant other or is it creating nothing more than a relationship of convenience? These questions and answers may also create a comfort zone if the answers received are satisfactory enough for a person to continue in the relationship. If a person tells another that they will stay true in a relationship, no matter what the other person does, depending upon the moral fortitude of the other person, they may just run out and cheat with anybody who will allow them to do so. Planning for the inevitable and improbable is one of the best yet most overlooked things people can do. When a group of friends go to a club, if there is a dress code and one or several members of that particular group are not allowed in, there is almost always an immediate idiot cluster, having a conversation, with the topic of discussion being; what are we gonna do now? Had the group planned for this possible adverse situation ahead of time, there would be no dumb discussions or hurt feelings on the part of the inadequately dressed individuals. Prior communication would have alleviated most or all of the unhappy feelings brought forth by the bouncer at the entrance to the club. If the group of partygoers would have made an agreement that either everybody goes in or nobody goes in, there would likely be no idiot cluster in front of the club. There would more likely be the sound of 'oh well we tried, let's hit a different spot.' Prior and ongoing communication is what people contemplating relationships, as well as those already in relationships need to be happy. Let each other know what each of you want and consistently strive to achieve it. This will alleviate many of the problems, which lack of communication will certainly bring.

Chapter Thirteen
The Dreaded Complacency

In relationships, as well as in almost all aspects of life there is one certainty. That certainty states that if anything is done without deviation for an extended period of time, eventually it will become boring. In fact it will become dreadfully complacent. The dreaded complacency is more than just boredom. It is what people who have no more drive or ambition in regards to their relationships experience. The dreaded complacency can resemble what some people consider love because many in relationships think that love, after a certain amount of time becomes routine. The main difference between love and complacency however is that love must remain new. A couple married ten years cannot exist happily solely on the memories from when the relationship was just starting out. The couple must constantly strive to make new memories on which to exist. When complacency enters a relationship, it's often hard to care about eradicating it because it usually makes a couple feel so darn comfortable. The comfortable state comes from predictability as in my husband comes home everyday and just reads the paper, then watches TV and then after dinner goes to sleep. The comfortable feeling can also come from the ways in which couples enjoy their intimate moments together as in 'we only go out on the weekends' or 'we only share intimacies on certain days and in certain ways.' Complacency is dreaded because there is often no escape. This is bad but what's worse is the fact that people know that their relationship has entered the dreaded complacency zone and they are helpless to do anything about it. Don't get me wrong, there are a lot of people who try to escape the confines of complacency but what usually ends up happening is one or both of the parties in the relationship attempts to recapture the infancy stages of the relationship where there is lustful infatuation and often reckless abandon. This may cause confusion because people sometimes believe that the new or renewed interest is due to infidelity – and this is because many times when a person in a relationship cheats, the home life seems to change. Complacency in my opinion is little more than getting to know a person too well. Once this happens, what else is there? The problem which speeds up the complacency process is the fact that people either give too much of themselves too quickly or they soon get to a point where they don't have anything else new to give. When complacency strikes, rather when complacency is known by the people involved in a relationship, it seems like it is too late to do anything about it. People try to circumvent it by dressing differently, trying new activities or the biggie, role-play. Role-play is a wonderful thing but it is best left to the young. When I say young I am not only speaking of those young in age as much as those young in the relationship. The big mistake people make in relationships that have ventured a little too far into the comfortable zone is that they want to be like they were when they were young. This cannot happen. Wait let me rephrase that - it can happen but with limited success. People in relationships sometimes get (for lack of a better word) 'tired' of seeing their partners. They know damn near everything about the ones they are connected to. This includes how this person smells, how this person looks naked, how this person reacts when certain body parts are stimulated and even how a person sounds when that person is having an orgasm. People mess up a lot with this role-play thing because they feel that by imagining the person they are in a relationship with is somebody else, automatically the sex will be better. Now I applaud the effort that these people are attempting to make but you have to realize how difficult this is. <u>A person cannot reinvent new.</u> When couples are just starting out and the idea of role-play enters the sexual arena, it should be embraced and explored as fully as possible but to be with someone for maybe ten, twenty or more years and to start dressing differently or acting like you don't know that person while you enact a meeting in a bar for the first time scene is little more than a waste of time. Why, because just as stated before, you already know what you are going to get. I do not want to sound like the pessimist here but how many times can a person make the same old thing into something new? 0. I do not want people to think that I am trying to persuade any one into thinking that infidelity or promiscuity is okay. I just want people to try and understand why some people choose these options. Let's look at this from a different angle. If a person buys a new pair of shoes or better yet a car and said person keeps the car for twenty years, the car may still work fine, it could even be upgraded with the latest gadgets and improvements – my question is wouldn't that person feel like he or she was missing out on something? This is what I believe to be human nature in its purest form. People are not bred to be used to only one thing. It may be because of poor moral values or because people are motivated by choice. Whatever the cause, variety is and always has been heavily desired as opposed to no choice at all. In relationships there is a time limit on new – ness. There will be a point when a person says to himself or the person he or she is involved in a relationship with – either directly or indirectly 'I'm tired of this – I want something new!' and it will not always be that the other person in the relationship is doing anything wrong, it could just be that the other has reached the point of 'I know so much about you - what else do you have to offer?' Many people in relationships rarely plan for the long term the way they do in other aspects of their lives. Let's look at finances for a second; people, smart people anyway, plan for adversity. They plan for education, marriage, family additions and so on. Many people even plan for retirement and by this I mean having enough money to live on once they stop working. In relationships, most people just say 'I'm just gonna jump into this with both feet and see where it takes me.' They figure that life will always provide the necessary stimulation and experiences to carry them along forever. They don't realize that there may actually be a point when there is nothing to talk about. If this were a case about money and the situation was a hypothetical stock market crash and a person instantly had no more resources, what would be the result? Well at the time this book went to print, we've already seen the result. People have taken their own lives; some of them have even taken the lives of their families because they had nowhere else to turn. Now granted, some may say that the comparison is a case of apples and oranges but in my opinion relationships rank right up there with employment. What is a person or couple to do when they get to that point where there is nothing left to do? I doubt seriously if anybody will resort to murder one to liven up an otherwise dead relationship but I am pretty sure that many other options for excitement will present themselves. This is where infidelity walks right in. The main reason people fear complacency so much is because if it comes, they know that sooner or later, the other party in the relationship will go looking for ways to eradicate it and I do not mean to say that the only way a person can eradicate complacency is through cheating but the fact that it is such a viable and available option is what has people nervous. People who become complacent in their relationships think that this is how love is and that this is how a relationship is supposed to be. When a person in a relationship introduces new ideas to combat the complacency, many times the belief is that the new ideas were or are brought about as a result of new interaction with someone else. Complacency causes people to get old prematurely because old people have a habit or history of not doing anything that young people do or anything which they themselves used to do when they were young. Complacency is almost the equivalent of being jaded in regards to new experiences. The best remedy or counter action for this is to never let this hindrance ease its way into your relationship. Continued spontaneity is great when trying to avoid complacency but what many people do is practice 'scheduled spontaneity.' They may go out every Friday or every second Saturday, when they should instead be going out whenever the mood hits and not to the same restaurants or same types of restaurants but every time try something new. This is a big world. Not embracing as much as this big world has to offer will lead to boredom and boredom is right down the block from complacency. A great many people or should I say scumbags will justify 'complacency based infidelity' as okay or quite common because it is something many people who have been in relationships for an extended period of time do. These people are wrong. Although there is an unwritten time limit on the initial euphoria in most relationships, there is none on fidelity. People can cheat after one week of being involved, just as easily as they can cheat after five years of togetherness. Neither situation makes it right or any better than the other. The fact that it happens means there are issues which need to be addressed. Those who say infidelity is destined to happen are nothing more than unhappy manipulators. There will always be unhappiness in relationships. There will not however always be infidelity as many manipulating people will try and have a person believe.

Chapter Fourteen
Marriage, Deception & Divorce

This world is built on and exists happily due to massive amounts of deception. I say this because as much as people desire and seek absolute truth, it is not the ultimate goal of most. What is the ultimate goal of most is happiness and to achieve happiness, many people like to believe that there must exist an equal amount of truth and deception. Truth often requires straightforwardness and harshness. Deception often includes ego stroking and straight up lying. The thing that many people in this world fail to realize is that everybody has an agenda and not only do they have an agenda, that agenda is not always the same agenda as that person's significant other. This is where compromise comes in. Now while the idea behind compromise is a good thing, it should be stated that there is a very fine line between it and deception. Compromise entails both parties giving up a little so that both parties can be happy. Deception sometimes means doing what I have to do in order to achieve a goal – up to and including compromise. Here's an example; a person in a relationship can go out partying every weekend. The partying person's significant other may not like or approve of this behavior at all. The partying person after realizing this may compromise and restrict the amount of going out if the significant other agrees to limit the amount of complaining. This may seem like a fair compromise but it can also be a form of deception if the partying person is just doing it so that he or she can enjoy un-aggravated time away from the significant other to go out and look for an affair. I know many will disagree with me but I believe this wholeheartedly; some deception is necessary in this world. Without deception, people would never be able to get a job. Without deception, people would never be able to have a relationship – or at least not a happy or long term one. Think about something - at the time of this book's printing, the minimum wage is somewhere about seven to eight dollars an hour. This is by no means an appropriate or adequate salary for a grown person to live on and definitely not an appropriate salary to raise a family. Yet many people do. The reason these people are able to live on this type of tip (I won't even call it a salary because the weekly amount is closer to a large tip than a salary) is because they have learned to live within or below their means. Think about something else; the tip, which this rate of pay provides is about the equivalent of $250 - $300 per week. If a person were to shop at these $0.99 stores, then that person would probably never have to worry about food again – especially when one can procure a box of rice, a can of beans and a drink for around $3. Using this type of logic and mathematical computation, if a person were to eat three meals a day, seven days a week, that person would be able to feed himself well for under seventy bucks. Add to that – if that person were to shop at the thrift stores which are prevalent in many communities, he would be able to definitely buy a decent number of clothes with the remaining funds and still have money for transportation and perhaps a movie or two. The only problem is that most of the people who work for minimum wage do not follow this pattern of behavior. They do not shop at $.99 stores nor do they shop at thrift or bargain basement type shops. They attempt to shop and eat like everybody else, which is why many of these people are either in bankruptcy court or housing court or experiencing some type of serious financial hardship. The reason they accept these sub standard paying jobs is because they need something as opposed to not having anything at all. Now I would like for all of you reading this to think about one more thing; if this individual had, at the interview for this illustrious minimum wage job told the interviewer the truth about what he wanted in regard to the job instead of what the interviewer wanted to hear, this individual would never have a job to begin with and would consequently be worse off than he already is. Everybody knows what this individual wanted to tell the interviewer in regard to what he wanted from the job; money. And not just a little bit of money but money to where this individual could take care of himself, his family, his bills, his hopes, dreams and aspirations. But you can't tell people that – why? Because most people know they cannot provide everything another person wants. You see, this person probably wanted to say to the interviewer 'I want the type of job which will afford me the opportunity to achieve every materialistic thing I can fathom' – which is what I honestly believe most of the people in this world actually want. The interviewer knows that he cannot provide these things and he also knows that he will not have to because if there ever was somebody who would actually have the gall to answer a question in such a manner, all that the interviewer would have to do is kindly kick that person out and offer the job to the next prospective client. This is why people play the lottery, this is why people fall victim to overnight million dollar money making schemes and this is why many people steal. They know that one person or one job will never provide them with what they truly desire. People say 'yes I want this job' when in actuality they are saying I need this job but as soon as something better comes along – screw you! With a capital F. Now apply this type of thinking to relationships; a person will more times than not accept what they truly do not desire just for the temporary benefits and immediate gratification it may provide. People will do this because they know full well that if they were to divulge the specifics of what they really want as in 'I just want somebody for sex and good home cooking' or 'I just want somebody to give me a child be cause this person looks like he or she will make a pretty baby' they would never be able to procure or maintain a relationship. Nobody in a relationship, no matter what they say, just wants to be used for one specific purpose even though many times it turns out that way. A relationship is many things and in a relationship people wear many hats. A person cannot be in a successful relationship and only cook or only provide sex or only take care of the kids. This is part of the deception that exists in many relationships. There are I believe thousands, maybe even hundreds of thousands of people that don't want to get married but who want to have sex – so just to achieve that goal they will marry the person they are courting who would not let them have sex until they were married. Then in a few months or a few years when the relationship fails people wonder why. There is really no need to wonder. People are not truthful. People are nice. A person who is not willing to hurt your feelings seems many times more desirable than someone who is capable of being brutally honest. In many relationships, people have this belief that whatever is wrong in the beginning will just work itself out over time. People believe this right up until the divorce proceedings. And the reason why is because they do not want to work on the relationship. They think that the relationship will one day wake up and take on a life of its own. When a person says this to himself, it is easy to see how absolutely ludicrous it sounds but this is what many in relationships expect. Here are a couple of for instances; if the sex between a new couple is less than stellar, instead of working on it people will just accept it and wish and hope and pray that it will get better. They will even make excuses and allowances for it when it doesn't as in 'a relationship is about so much more than just sex.' Now this is true, relationships are about much more than sex but many of the people using this excuse are not being truthful and consequently not being made happy. This creates long term deception and that's not good. Long term deception creates or contributes to fake relationships and fake relationships contribute to someone often trying to remove that person from the face of the earth. Here's another example; a person may say that he or she loves kids, especially those of the person that this individual is interested in but this needn't be necessarily true. People put up with children they would otherwise not because there is something to be gained by doing so. This something could be a long term relationship with the parent of the kids or maybe just a sexual relationship with the parent of these kids. The problem is basically as I mentioned above, people are not truthful, people are nice and the bad thing about this is that eventually the truth will eradicate the niceness. I said earlier that I believed a little deception was necessary in relationships and I still stand by that statement but the deception I speak of is necessary only for temporary peace and happiness – or should I say satisfactory peace and happiness. The reason I believe some deception is necessary is because in today's world, more often than not, people are looking for perfection. People are not looking for fixer uppers, people are looking for someone who will be everything they ever wanted and who will continue to be so until the relationship is over. Many women in today's world do not want to hear a man they are interested in say 'I'm not perfect but I will try to be and do everything you would want your perfect man to be and do.' And the reason is because many of these women don't like the word try. To them, the word try means to fail. It means that a man is somehow incapable of being everything that this woman needs. Sometimes people are hurt so bad in one relationship that they desire to eradicate all possibility of hurt in subsequent relationships and the easiest way rather one of the easiest ways to do this is to not get into relationships or raise the bar in regard to what they want in relationships so high that every potential suitor will fall short. This is why people are sometimes deceptive. They know in their hearts that they will never completely be what you want so they act the part long enough to get theirs. What more people in today's relationships need but don't have is brutal and complete honesty. And by this I do not mean for a person to say to his or her partner 'I like you with long hair as opposed to short hair' or 'I like it when you serve me breakfast in bed.' I mean a person should be able to say 'I don't like the way you have sex' or 'I don't approve of the way you dress' or even 'I don't like the type of company you keep, even if they are your best friends.' And that person should be able to say these things without fear of reprisal from the significant other because the significant other knows that the possibility exists that whatever the other says just might be true. Brutal and complete honesty extends from the good end of the spectrum all the way to the bad. The problem with this is that people are more willing to be completely and brutally honest when the news is good but when it comes to the not so good; people feel they need to soften the blow before the blow is given. This leads to people not saying all they really mean or all they really need to say. Brutal and complete honesty leads to absolute trust. I like to believe that absolute trust leads to if not happiness, then complete understanding. If people had complete understanding of one another, there would be no arguments, no fights and definitely no divorce. But just like there will always be marriages, there will always be the opposite end of the spectrum. If people would mention to one another each and every time that person made them upset or every time that person did something that the other just did not like, this would be a wonderful world. But we know this will never happen and this is why deception will always be a part of this world. Some people in this world cannot stand to hurt other people's feelings and some people in this world cannot stand to have their feelings hurt. What happens when these two types of people get together? They do whatever they can to not hurt one another up to and including lying to make each other believe that they are perfect. This brings us to an inevitable divorce...or altercation. Divorce by definition means an ending of a marriage by an official decision in a court of law. This does not mean that a couple actually falls out of love with one another, it means that said couple desires to remove themselves from the contract of marriage. Now just like with marriage people divorce themselves for many reasons. The most popular being because they hate each other. There are other reasons such as infidelity, irreconcilable differences and there is even the sexual incompatibility issue. Sometimes people divorce because they tire of one another and sometimes they do it simply because there's somebody else they want to marry. Divorce, just like marriage is never simple. It always costs something and it always causes something. We all know it costs money, whether to retain an attorney or whether to pay the settlement that the opposing attorney has helped the other party reach. What many people who get divorced as well as those who decide to involve themselves with these people don't always know is that a divorce can often bring about feelings of resentment toward the opposite sex, which can last for life. In short, it is one of the worst things that can happen to a marriage. It is sometimes like punitive damages. I say this because when most people divorce they want to hurt one another as payback for everything that went wrong during the marriage. There was a time when people who fell out of love with one another wanted little or nothing at all to do with the person they were no longer in love with. But now people use divorce to get back at the other party the same way many women use child support to get back at a man who has hurt them. The whole idea of divorce, which I have seemingly and mistakenly come to the conclusion as being a mutual parting of the ways and an equal division of the assets has been misconstrued, twisted and basically made into 'get all you can from this bitch!' Divorce is eerily similar to punitive damages because it is not usually just a plan of separation. It is often a form of punishment. It can even be seen as a form of coercion to make people do good. Think about something; if a person commits a traffic infraction, depending upon the seriousness of infraction, that person will receive a ticket. If that person does not respond to the ticket, that person will have to pay money as a form of punishment. If a person liters and gets caught, there is also a fine. If a person attempts to take the subway in NYC and does not pay the required fare, guess what, another fine. The one thing that all these infractions have in common is the fact that the end result will cost a person some money. In many court cases there's what's called punitive damages. These are damages that are awarded by a court to punish the defendant rather than to compensate the victim or compensate the victim by punishing the defendant. This means that a person or company will have to pay another money for wrongs, which have been caused. This is one of those things, which scares people away from commitment. Commitment always comes with the possibility of failure – and this is a reasonable yet much overlooked expectation. Too many people think that when they involve themselves in a relationship, the relationship will never end and it will always be wonderful. – Silly them! The idea behind punitive damages is basically how people scare others into being good. Christianity for example has the belief that if you sin during your time on earth and die within your sin, your soul will be subject to an eternal torment, which means forever! Since nobody in his or her right mind would really want to suffer an eternal torment, this belief could be simply looked at as a way to scare others into being good. Now let's look at divorce. Divorce or the prospect of is what makes certain people either get into marriages or run from the possibility of them at full speed. The main reason being because people are not true with their intentions anymore. Many people today want to get married to someone who is financially secure so that after a couple of months or after a couple of years, they can get detached and automatically become comfortable due to the wonderfully conniving attorney that they have retained. People in this world are not stupid. They know or can see the potential for greatness so to speak in the people they get involved with. Sometimes these people, seeing that there is great potential for the other to make great sums of money, will get involved until the other makes great sums of money, then will divorce that person under the guise of 'I was with you when you had nothing so I deserve half!' This is what causes fear. Nobody really knows what's on the mind of another person, therefore many people are hesitant about pursuing a relationship – whether a person has a multitude of resources or not. The fact that a person can lose a home or lose his or her financial security just because he or she falls in love with someone is more than enough reason to make that person shy away from the prospect of relationships. The one thing about a relationship that many people overlook is the fact that it is little more than two people working together to keep the relationship together. Don't believe me? Ask anybody what happens in a relationship when one person decides to stop caring. It's pretty simple – the relationship <u>will</u> fail. This does not necessarily mean marriage. This means any relationship. This means that for a relationship to last, whatever is done is done for the betterment and benefit of both parties. People have this illusion that just because a couple is married, that couple loves each other more than a couple who is just boyfriend and girlfriend. These people are wrong. Love does not entail paperwork. Never has, never will. There is nowhere that says a person has to be married to be happy. There is however the stipulation that if you are a religious and or righteous person, to be in sync with the laws of most religions, marriage is necessary – especially if one plans to consummate that relationship. There is this belief that people are not truly happy unless they get married. They feel that marriage is the culmination of a couple's love for one another. I must say that to an extent I agree but only to an extent. Marriage, just like everything else in this world is a choice. A person has the choice to do good, just as that person has the choice to do bad. A person has the choice to succeed in life, just as that person has the choice to fail. Marriage is what many people in this world have commercialized and sensationalized a happy relationship into aspiring to. It's kinda like the mother's and father's day thing where people have to go out and buy – wait, let me rephrase that. It's kinda like the mother and father's day thing where people are forced to go out and buy things to prove their love to their parents. Do not get me wrong, I see very little wrong with showing love to the people who raised you and if they did a good job, I believe every gratuity and appreciation should be bestowed upon them. I just don't believe it can only be done on that one particular day. What if you are the type of person who lives paycheck to paycheck and has difficulty in keeping a steady job and were to lose your job a couple of weeks before the above mentioned holidays? Would that mean that you love your parents any less just because you could not afford to buy them that big ole flat screen or that diamond pendant? Of course not. But this is what society has deemed a crime. You have to do what everybody else does otherwise you are not as good as everybody else. With marriage many times there are what I like to call miscommunications. By this I mean people will get involved with one another for an unspecified amount of time. This can stretch anywhere from a few months to a few years. This is not uncommon or abnormal. What people do while they are in these relationships for months and years and centuries and eons is not completely examine where each of them wants the relationship to go and in what fashion. This again is not uncommon or abnormal because in most relationships, if there are no problems or seemingly few reasons for arguments, why would people want to change? (You know the old don't mess with what works) But this is exactly the thing, which causes problems. Many women are taught that they have to be married and this is because only bad girls sleep around – whether it be with one or whether it be with many. This belief is often instilled in women by parents, girlfriends, religious institutions and the media. So to avoid being labeled a bad girl quite often the women will make getting married their ultimate goal. This is not such a bad thing. What is a bad thing is the fact that these women attempt to procure that commitment for reasons other than love. They do it because their girlfriends are doing it or because their parents are doing it and their parents will accept nothing less than what they themselves have done or they do it because they feel that this is what has to be done. On the opposite side of the coin, many men are taught that all women just want to get married so that they can have their fantasy wedding and basically end up changing the life of the man into a position of new age slavery and submission. This belief is instilled in these men from fathers, brothers and friends who have had relationships with the above types of women. So to avoid being the type of man that this type of relationship is sure to bring, quite often the men make avoiding marriage their ultimate goal. This is not a bad thing. The bad thing is that these men do not always tell the women how they actually feel and end up lying to the women to make their relationship focus resemble that of the women. This is miscommunication! People get involved because they think that they are on the same wavelength but the paths are going in two separate directions. One wants to get married but the other one doesn't. When people get together and don't set guidelines or ground rules, then the relationship will just exist until the day of its death. I do not mean to imply that a woman should say 'I want to be married by April 10th of next year otherwise I'm leaving you!' I mean that if a woman wants to be married she should let it be known with an approximate date when she gets into a relationship. For instance, 'I know there is no textbook timeframe for marriage but personally I would like to be married by the time I'm forty.' (this works better if the woman is around 35 or 36) four to five years, in my opinion should be enough time for a person to adequately know if he or she wants to marry the person he or she is involved with. If a woman is younger, then she can say after a number of years; I believe you are the person I want to spend my life with and I want to marry you. This puts the ball in the man's court because he will have the option to say yes or the task of explaining why not. With a lot of men, if they do not desire to get married, they will prolong the act for as long as possible. (If you're gonna get the milk for free, why buy the cow?) Women know this and this is why they will throw the 'when are we getting married' question into the equation when they have been together for a while but see no light at the end of the tunnel. This is also one of the reasons why guys say women change or have ulterior motives. People do not always talk to the person they are involved with the way they should. They will hide things because they feel its better to keep the truth away from someone for fear of hurting their feelings as opposed to taking the chance on telling the truth and letting the chips fall where they may. People need to eradicate miscommunication. They need to talk long, hard and often about what they desire, what they are feeling and especially what they are thinking. The problem with this is that people do talk but they talk to everybody except those who actually matter and in most relationships the only two people who matter are the two people involved with one another. Once people in relationships know what they want, they can communicate that to the other party in the relationship and this will more often than not effectively eradicate much of the miscommunication in relationships today. It will also erase much of the fear that the consequences of divorce and separation can provide.

End